Adventures of a Young Preacher

Dr. Charles A. Crane
2018

Adventures of A Young Preacher
is available at special quantity discounts for bulk purchase for sales promotions,
premiums, fund-raising, and educational needs.
For details write Endurance Press, 577 N Cardigan Ave Star, ID 83669.

Visit Endurance Press' website at www.endurancepress.com

Adventures of A Young Preacher

PUBLISHED BY ENDURANCE PRESS
577 N Cardigan Ave
Star, ID 83669 U.S.A.

All rights reserved. Except for brief excerpts for review purposes,
no part of this book may be
reproduced or used in any form without
prior written permission from the publisher.

ISBN 978-0-998875644

®2018 Dr. Charles A Crane

Cover Design by Janet Colburn

Printed in the United States of America

First Edition 2018

Contents

An Introduction 5
Douglas County, Oregon 9
A Man Named Paul Carruthers 11
An Unwise Pledge 13
Why Did God Put Skunks in Such a Pretty Place? 15
Confidence? 17
Ministerial Hospitality 21
Sister-in-Law 25
His Name Was Blackie 29
Ministerial Embarrassments and Baptismal Blunders 33
The Andreesons 35
Associate Ministers 37
Mr. VFW 41
Yellow Creek 45
Do You Understand What Makes Babies? 51
House Calls 55
Eloquent Profanity Leads to Praise 59
Bernard and Benevolence 63
It Was a Winning Season 65
Making Ladies Beautiful 67
Union Gap 69
Unbelievable Power 71
Pray About Everything 75
Chief Crumley Gives Advice 79
The Brothers 81
Sisters Cut from a Similar Cloth 87
Broken Body, Mended Spirit 95
Marrying Sam 99
You've Got My Full Cooperation 103
A Few Rough Edges 105
The Ravens of God 111
"I Can't Do Much But I Can Make Money" 117
Hoof in Mouth Disease 121
The Lennial Reigns 125

Brother Fred's Pants	129
The Parsonage	131
Summer Camp and the Crow's Nest	141
The Crow's Nest	142
Competition	144
Campfire	144
Elijah and the Prophets of Baal	145
The Value of Christian Camping	146
Camp Christian Colorado	146
Think You Would Like to Travel?	149
Zimbabwe	151
On Location	156
Feeding the Physical Body	158
Results	159
Chidamoya Compound	160
Mono Pools	166
Meaning	172
Ministry and Travel	175
David	175
Ned	177
Egypt	181
An Interest that Began at Age Thirteen	185
Homer	185
Sally	186
Lowel	187
Larry	188
Dean	188
Lamar the Banker	189
"We just think we should visit a Christian Church before we are baptized in the Mormon Church."	194
The Missionaries at the Door	196
A Mission President and University President	197
A Young Couple Seeks the Truth	199
An Old Seventh-Day Adventist	200
Capstone Conference	201
Judge for Yourself	203

An Introduction

Do preachers really wear starched underwear and sleep in straight jackets? Is their favorite fruit persimmon? Do they have a negative moral judgment about every subject? Do they ever laugh or have a sense of humor? Is black their favorite color? Do they wear a white shirt and tie when they sleep? Are all preachers a bit substandard in IQ, rather bumbling idiots? Does anyone really understand what goes on in the mind (public and personal life) of a minister? Are they really like they are usually portrayed on television or in the movies? Unfortunately, the above depiction is the way preachers are often portrayed by the media.

Have preachers and ministry been understood? Could it be that one of the world's most significant professions needs some public relations work done on its behalf? Most likely the public has significant misconceptions of one of the world's greatest and most rewarding professions.

Of three leading professions—teaching, medicine, and the ministry, teaching trains the mind, medicine cares for the body, but ministry serves the soul, body-mind-spirit of man. The mind and body are temporary, only the spiritual part is eternal.

In reality the preaching ministry is filled with excitement, challenge, opportunity, and many experiences that to the general public seem almost unbelievable. Almost any moment of any day has the potential for events to transpire that lead the preacher off in interesting encounters—some almost beyond belief.

There are those "in-season times" and many "out-of-season" times. Viewing these circumstances from a humorous perspective can lead to times of almost uncontrollable mirth.

These experiences, blended together, form the basis of a life of advantage and usefulness to mankind. People are encouraged and directed, or redirected towards productive lives. Many are led to a total new birth in their existence.

The following short stories are usually not autobiographical in nature, but look towards the people served rather than the author. The purpose is to demonstrate the value and usefulness of the preacher's life. Sometimes the stories are biographical, although that is not the main point of the stories. It is my hope that ministry might be seen in a more reliable perspective than has sometimes been portrayed in the media.

The ministry often is a life of mystery, challenge, and excitement. True, a person frequently needs a sense of humor to survive in some situations, but this is true of most professions.

It helps if one loves people deeply and has a strong desire to serve others. If these traits are present, the ministry provides many unequaled opportunities for fulfillment.

Oh yes, as with all professions, there is plenty of hard work. In the end the satisfaction of a job well done and seeing people genuinely helped offer rewards far beyond monetary goals. In hard times or easy times, there are the people. People make it all worthwhile. Working with people can be more fascinating than almost anything else in the entire world.

Ministry is a frontier to explore; there are conquests of humanity, civilization, unexplored vistas of the mind and soul patiently awaiting someone with the will to seek and explore. It is hoped that an inside view of the ministry might entice daring, worthy souls to seek out its mysteries and challenges.

Each reader will need to judge in their own minds the value and meaning of these events. Have they made the preacher's life purposeful and useful? Ask yourself: Were not many people helped? Were not many people changed—and for the better? Were not these people's eternal destinies changed? Was not this work more important than building a bridge or house?

Some of the stories are humorous, some sad, some unbelievable, but all of them are true. In some cases the names have been changed and the exact places disguised to protect good people who might be embarrassed by their story being given publicity.

Some of the stories have been blended together from earlier or later events in ministry, since the subject matter is similar. Yet each of these events happened someplace, sometime, and to a preacher and the people he served. These are all true stories.

Douglas County, Oregon

The earth is filled with beautiful places, but to a native of Douglas County, Oregon, it must appear the most beautiful spot on earth. Even to one who was not born there it must rate high as one of the places on which God took very special pains in creation.

In the southeast corner of the county lies Crater Lake National Park. The lake lies in a volcanic crater on top of what was once Mt. Mazama. In some distant age past, the mountain blew off its top and left behind one of the deepest and bluest lakes on earth. The drive around the rim of Crater Lake reveals one breathtaking vista after another. It is not uncommon to see deer, bear, even an occasional elk in the grassy meadows during the late spring, summer, or early fall. The rest of the year the lake and roads are snowed in and can only be visited by snowmobiles, snowshoe, or helicopter. It is one of the scenic wonders of the world.

Just below and to the north is Diamond Lake. Diamond Lake is surrounded by mountain peaks and pine forests. The fishing in Diamond Lake is probably one of the best of many fine lakes in Oregon. Its near-perfect conditions for the growth of trout means it often is a place where fishing becomes the experience of a lifetime.

Diamond Lake provides the headwaters for one of the most beautiful rivers of the northwestern United States—the North Umpqua. The Umpqua got its name from an Indian tribe. It also is noted for its remarkable fishing. Twenty-five miles of the upper river are limited to fly fishing only. Such noted outdoorsmen as

Zane Gray loved this magnificent river. Zane Gray owned a cabin at the forks of the North Umpqua and Steamboat Creek.

The Cascade Mountains are covered with Douglas fir trees. There still remain millions of acres of virgin timber on the western slopes of the Cascades. This is the setting into which the following stories fit. The beauty of this area will hopefully be blended into the events that transpired.

A Man Named Paul Carruthers

One of the men of our small town in Douglas County was named Paul Carruthers. He was a logger. He was not one to keep up his yard or house. It looked rather like he was planning to sell junk after he retired from logging to subsidize his Social Security check.

His wife came to church occasionally, and one day in passing, mentioned that Paul had developed a special fishing fly that would lure the crafty trout of the upper Umpqua. She said, "Charles, if you would come out and talk fishing with Paul you might get him to come to church."

Well, I didn't get him out to church, but the visit wasn't fruitless, as Paul gave me several of his special "caddis" flies. They were the best dry fly I ever tried.

On the opening day of fishing on the North Umpqua there are so many fishermen that one is said to "need to take their own rock to stand on." It isn't really quite that bad, but people come from far and near to fish the turquoise waters.

My friend Rodney Leatherwood and I were there plenty early to find a special hole that we had scouted out well in advance. We were the first there due to having gotten up not too long after going to bed.

I waded out into the rushing water that was coming down out of the snow. The water is normally clear, but on this day it was especially crystalline. Few rivers are more beautiful. The blue-green color is beyond description; even photos do not do it justice.

I caught fish on nearly every cast with the caddis fly until it was coming unraveled, and continued to catch them when the fly had disintegrated until about two inches of material was stringing out behind it.

After catching and releasing many fish I came out of the river with the nicest limit of trout caught that day. I had been having so much fun that I had not realized just how cold the water was, and it took two weeks to get rid of the chilblains in my legs.

The North Umpqua is joined downriver by the South Umpqua at the town of Roseburg. The south river is not nearly as large or beautiful as the North. Together they run on through Douglas County to the coast at Reedsport. The river has its beginning and ending all in Douglas County.

This remarkable day of fishing was a fringe benefit of seeking to speak to Paul Carruthers about his spiritual needs. Although he never came to church he did keep me supplied with an incredible fly for fishing. Fishing for souls led to a good days fishing on the river.

An Unwise Pledge

Jack Defoe and Bill Joslin were some very dedicated fishermen. Each spring the salmon would run up the Umpqua River to spawn. Jack and Bill were usually there to meet them.

In the spring of '62 they made a covenant that they would not return to church until they had caught a Chinook salmon. Both were young and in what they thought was perfect health. They worked hard in the woods and neither was given to habits of dissipation or excess.

Jack was supposed to be a Christian and Bill wasn't much of anything. Jack said one day, "Well, God made these fish, and He can help us catch them. Let's make a deal that we won't return to church until we have caught a salmon each." They shook on the bargain. It was a bad deal, and I'm sure they both knew it at the time—yet they agreed.

That Lord's day they caught nothing. The next Lord's day they caught nothing. On the following Sunday Bill said to Jack, "Jack, I don't feel so well. I am nauseated, my arms feel sort of weak, and they hurt." He had no more than finished these words when he fell over dead in the boat. He was only 34 years old.

Jack was man enough to tell of his part in the complicity. It was a warning to our little community that one does not threaten God. Unfortunately, lessons learned like this often are not remembered too long. It was a sad time for the church, the family, and friends. The whole community grieved.

Even a fine thing like fishing can be bad when it takes the place of one's responsibility to God and family.

Why Did God Put Skunks in Such a Pretty Place?

Did you ever wonder why God made skunks? There are even skunks in Israel where the Creator lived His human life. Well, skunks have definitely discovered Douglas County. On a warm spring night the essence of their exploits can frequently be smelled.

One of the deacons from the church had purchased a fine new car. (Over the years people have insisted that I drive their new Buicks, Cadillacs, Infinitys, etc.) But this new Ford was his pride and joy. It was shiny black and beautiful. He was so proud of it that he insisted that I take it to deliver some teenagers home after a church social. I rather reluctantly accepted the keys after saying, "Kent, I'd feel awful if I put a scratch on it or something."

Sure enough, something awful did happen. We had headed out west on Central Street and were making good time in the luxury of the fine new piece of machinery when suddenly out of the ditch came a large skunk all set to do business with the preacher and the deacon's new Ford. The worst had happened—the skunk was dead, but the Ford smelled very much alive.

Can you imagine my embarrassment when I had to take back Kent's new car which, for the next month, would bear distinct evidence of its encounter with the striped kitty with the fluid drive?

Douglas County, Oregon is one of the many places on this earth that shows evidence of the handiwork of the Creator. There, as everywhere on earth, man must take his place in God's plan for the earth and his life. Young or old, we each must recognize God in what He has made and submit our lives to Him. Douglas

Adventures of a Young Preacher

County helped me to understand the power and grandeur of our Creator.

Confidence?

He did not have the ability to instill confidence. Why, was not clear at first—only it wasn't there from the start. He was a large, sort of pudgy man. His hair was graying and was usually worn in a grown-out crew cut, two to three weeks past needing cutting. I often wondered how he kept it so it always looked like it needed to be cut. His horned-rim glasses were usually a bit down on his nose. He wore shoes with thick soft rubber soles that always needed polish, and he often sucked on an unlit pipe like it filled some long ago unmet need.

His office had all of the equipment of the era. The seats were soft green cushions with chrome pipe frames that had been popular in doctor's office some twenty years earlier.

The office had asphalt tile on the floor, usually needing mopping and waxing. There was a lamp that gave off a purple light that was thought to kill the germs brought in by all the sick people. There was the smell of medicine and dust. This was my impression on my first and successive visits to his office.

One of the hazards of being a minister is talking too much that results in a sore throat. As a young minister it wasn't long till I had a sore throat. This had developed into a full-blown case of bronchial infection. At the suggestion of one of our members, Kathryn, who was a registered nurse, I made a trip over to Dr. Fredricks' office.

His words were, "So, you're the new Reverend in town?" I responded hoarsely, "Well, I'm at least the new preacher; I don't feel very reverend today."

He said, "Well, come on in and let me take a look at you." With some humming and thumping on my chest, listening to my breathing, examining my throat, nose, and ears finally said, "Was college hard for you?" I assured him that it had been and I was glad it was over. He replied, "Well, I had a devil of a time getting through medical school myself. I didn't learn most of what they taught us. Frankly, I'm surprised they gave me a degree. Always wondered if they made a mistake?" still up close examining me, talking with the pipe clenched between his teeth.

Further encounters with dear Doc Fredricks did not increase my confidence. Many stories about his confidence-robbing statements floated around our town. Really though, he was not too bad as a doctor.

Our church building was not yet completed and did not have a baptistery. This necessitated our borrowing one from another church or going to the river. We tried using other churches' baptisteries and found them to be either dirty, empty when needed, or hard to schedule.

A young lady came to accept Christ one Sunday evening and the church leaders decided to go to a place out Calapooya Creek to baptize. We made the trip to what was a nearly perfect place. It was back from the road where the creek cut through rich soil and passed through the midst of a large grove of oak trees.

The water was clear and safe for swimming. We were preparing for baptism with a 4x4 pickup's lights shining on the spot where the baptism was to take place.

I was just ready to enter the water when a scream of panic and pain rang out nearby. The baptism was temporarily postponed while we checked out what had happened. When we found the source of the cries it turned out to be one of the young mothers, Darla Redding.

She had experienced a sudden call of nature and thought she could slip off through the bushes to a safe spot in the dark. Due to the darkness she did not realize that she was squatting on the brink of a small bank that dropped twenty feet to the rocks below. The bank had caved away and she had fallen over the bank.

Although she was injured she was insisting that no one come near her or shine a light on her. With her injury she was having difficulty getting her clothes back on. We dispatched a lady to help her regain her modesty. One of the men who was 6-foot-6 tall and very strong carried this chunky little gal out to where the 4x4 was parked.

When she had been made as comfortable as possible we continued quickly with the baptism. The people from the church proceeded as a group to Dr. Fredrick's office in town some five miles away.

While they waited at the doctor's office I rounded up the doctor and he and I were examining Darla's leg. To my untrained eye it looked obviously broken. At the knee it stuck out to the side at a 90 degree angle.

Our dear doctor began to hum and thump. Finally he said, "I really don't know what is wrong." I replied, "It has to be broken doesn't it?"

"Well, yes, I guess it does. I will have to go get a medical book and try to see if we can find out anything."

In a short while he returned and opened the book right on top of Darla's stomach. She was laying on her back in pain on the examining table. He then began to search and search back and forth through the pages and finally in frustration said, "Well, I don't know what is wrong with her leg. Guess you will have to take her to Roseburg to the hospital."

Sure enough, the leg was broken. Darla was in a cast and on crutches for weeks. We had many a laugh about our dear doctor not recognizing a broken leg.

Dr. Fredricks had many fine points and for routine medical things he was just fine; especially if you knew what was wrong with you and what you wanted done for it.

During these lean years of ministry he treated our whole family without charge. If something serious was wrong he would send us over to the bigger city and to a specialist. But Dr. Fredricks offered a real service to the community and the church because of his generous nature. It was another way God made it possible for us to live on the modest pay we received starting out in ministry.

We immediately saw the need of a baptistery in the church, and in a few weeks one was completed and was used frequently for the remainder of our ministry there.

I often wondered if Dr. Fredricks was as poor a doctor as he portrayed—really he was quite competent. Stories circulated around the community that led me to believe that he was really quite a good doctor but had a way of giving an impression of incompetence.

Ministerial Hospitality

Personal relationships are potentially filled with opportunities for blessings or possibly disaster. Unfortunately the events surrounding the sisters-in-law had been building like a great storm. Something should be done, but what? Such was the case of the crisis with the sisters-in-law.

After Bible college and ordination we were called to be interviewed by the previously-mentioned small rural Oregon church in Douglas County. There had been a long list of ministerial candidates of which we were number nine of the preacher parade.

There had also been a long list of hospitality candidates for the prospective new minister. This list and the list of ministerial candidates had been exhausted except for one remaining name on each of the lists—ours and Frieda's. We were scheduled for a noon meal at her home following the morning church services. I'm glad we had no idea what awaited us.

Clues that this was not to be a cultural or culinary highlight of our lives were not long in forthcoming. As we approached the given address, a variety of cats and dogs were bounding into and out of the driveway. The driveway was filled with large puddles and surrounded by a decaying fence.

The yard was overgrown with evergreen briars, which grow profusely in western Oregon. Up the drive stood a rundown shack where, we learned later, Freida and her henpecked husband lived. Neither professed to be Christians.

Our first impression of Freida was that she was a good candidate for a character role in a second-rate western movie. She

Adventures of a Young Preacher

was short and squatty, with sparse graying hair sticking out in all directions from her head. A cigarette dangled loosely from her lips, with a long ash hanging at the end.

It soon became apparent that she would as soon swear at someone as talk to them. In fact, she didn't even realize she was swearing. She said what was on her mind no matter where or when.

In her face could be seen anger and evidence of a life of immoderation and dissipation. She seemed at the same time friendly, yet hostile; smiling, yet belligerent. I said quietly to my wife, "This situation has promise of becoming interesting." She was not so sure.

We were greeted at the door by Freida's rather brash words, "Well, come in, you can't eat out in the yard. I know this dump ain't much, but if we can live here all the time you should be able to stand it for a couple of hours."

Inside we were greeted by chickens, a dog, several cats, and even a small pig. The odor was in keeping with the surroundings. The furniture had long since seen its better days and probably had long ago been purchased from a charitable used furniture store, or maybe picked up from the garbage dump.

Freida had to shoo the animals out of the house. Her husband, Willard, who had not been to church that morning, came in the back door and greeted us with, "I don't have much time for religion, but Freida goes to church some, even though she shore don't live it here at home."

She reprimanded him with, "What do you know about anything? Why don't you shut up or try to say something intelligent for a change!"

Freida then said, "Well, I had my name on that list for over two months and I guess they didn't want to send anybody out here. I had forgotten that I had even signed up until they sent you home with me today. I guess I had better see if I can fix something to eat."

The furniture was covered with the leavings of the chickens, cats and other animals. A rather mildewed looking sheet was spread over the couch so we could sit and watch while lunch was being prepared. We would have been better off not watching.

She began the preparations by taking her soiled sleeve and wiping off the very dirty counter where the chickens had been roosting or cat sleeping. She began to roll out the noodles for chicken and noodles as ashes fell from her cigarette.

She said to us, "I don't know if you are going to like what I fix, but if you don't you can just go hungry."

A favorite saying among my father and his brothers had been, "Chicken is too close a relative to a Crane to eat." I had grown up with this idea firmly implanted in my mind. Chicken was the one food that to me was intolerable.

Finally, after an hour and a half the meal was ready. Freida said, "Well, come and get it or I will throw it to the pigs."

The chicken seemed almost alive as I struggled to swallow it. Nevertheless, we ate what was set before us, asking no questions. We did not become ill. That first day almost ended my desire to be a preacher.

Over the next several months we grew to love Freida and Willard.

Later Freida gave her life to the Lord; Willard to my knowledge never did.

Both have many years since passed away. God used our discomfort for good.

The children became Christians, and one daughter graduated from Bible college.

Sister-in-law

The vote to be called as the new preacher for the church came after an intensive interview in which the only question asked of me was, "Does your wife play the piano?" This began what was a most satisfying and productive ministry among the beautiful Christian people of Douglas County.

A few weeks after beginning our work I was asked to call on a lady named "Hilda." She was recognized as a real fright by the people of the community. Her claim to notoriety was that she had "cleaned the plow" of several men.

She worked in a lumber mill where most people, including the men, would not dare cross her. She was gruff and tough, large and raw boned. She knew how to intimidate people, men or women—especially the young preacher.

I began to worry about the call almost as soon as I promised one of the church members that I would visit her. On the appointed day I had a quivering feeling in the bottom of my stomach and a profusion of underarm perspiration as well as clammy hands.

Her first words were, "Well, was it that worthless sister-in-law who sent you over here to pester me? I'm too busy and have worthwhile things to do instead of wasting my time going to church."

By this time I was wishing I could slip out, but Hilda was firmly in control, so I made a sincere effort to be cordial. I said, "Well, I'm new here in town trying to get acquainted with everyone. If you don't mind I would like to visit with you a few minutes. I promise I won't invite you to church."

I learned that our hostess of the chicken and noodles affair, Freida and Hilda were sisters-in-law. They got along so poorly that they even preferred to shop on alternate days at the grocery store in this small town.

The truth was that Freida had not asked me to visit Hilda. When she saw Hilda at church she had some choice words about her, indicating that she was far beyond the reach of the Lord.

Things ran smoothly for a few weeks. Then a town meeting was called to discuss whether the community should build a public swimming pool. At the meeting Freida was for the swimming pool and Hilda against it. Freida still had children at home and Hilda didn't. Hilda hated swimming for reasons to be learned later.

The fracas started when disagreements turned to insults, insults to swearing at each other, swearing to bodily threats, and threats to blows. Soon hair and clothes were flying as they snatched each other nearly naked.

The whole town was abuzz with the story. Of course Freida came out the loser of the battle, but not before she had inflicted some serious pain on Hilda.

Does this really make ministry glamorous? The story does not end here. Freida was first to yield to the Savior. Her disposition showed remarkable improvement. The saying was true of her, "She wasn't what she had been, but still was not what she should be." The Lord did make remarkable progress in her needy life.

The church, and community, were astounded a few months later when Hilda came to Christ. Hilda was so afraid of water that she wouldn't even live in a house with a bathtub in it.

After weeks of study and my earning her confidence she was finally baptized. I asked her one day, "Hilda, what is it that keeps you from being baptized?"

She said, "I guess you thought I wasn't afraid of anything, but when I was a child my brothers beat up on me constantly. That is how I learned to fight. Twice they held me under water until I was unconscious. I have had a deathly fear of water ever since." It was a victory of faith for her to be baptized.

Both ladies have since gone to be with the Lord. Both came from lives of anger and heartache to know the redeeming power of Jesus.

How often have we laughed and talked of Hilda and Freida and what they meant to our lives. What would have been their ends if we had not come into theirs?

Can you imagine my feeling of satisfaction when a couple of years later Hilda was teaching Sunday school, at peace with herself and God? I could not hold back a few tears of joy.

His Name Was Blackie

About five months after ordination and three months after accepting the charge of my first church, we were settling into the parsonage. It had been a parsonage for many years and showed the many signs of constant use and very occasional or deferred maintenance. Remind me to tell you about that later.

Everything was going well, but how does one get the confidence of a community that has seen preachers come and go every two or so years as long as they can remember? Two more years, and then what, is their thought.

It must be that God not only looks out for fools and children, but also young preachers who are really trying to do their job. It was true in this case for sure.

One of the ladies of the church, Dolores O'Malley, said, "I have been trying to help one of our neighbors, and could use a little help from you. Would you visit them? They are old and really in bad shape physically and spiritually."

I was not prepared for what I saw. When I came to the door, Mrs. Avis said, "Come in, but you may be getting into more than you would want to if you knew the whole situation." She seemed disturbed and unhappy. Her next words were, "Well, I guess you come to see Blackie. He's in the bedroom. Come on in."

Blackie, whose real name I was to find out later was Howard, had apparently suffered a stroke some time back and was limited to a wheelchair or bed. There was deep hostility between he and his wife. It was not long in being demonstrated.

Howard said, "Do you see what kind of a mess I live in here? She won't do anything for me." She replied, "Well, if he treated you like he does me, would you do anything for him?"

What happened next I had not been prepared for by any class in college. Howard, with his left hand—his right hand was paralyzed—threw his ashtray at her, barely missing her head and ricocheting it off the wall. She made a hasty retreat out of the room, and I continued to talk with Blackie.

I asked him how he had come up with the name Blackie. He said he and Anna had only been married a few years. Before that time he was a logger, chased women, drank hard liquor, and fought more men than any other man in the country. At the time I thought it was just big talk. Later I learned it was true. From the time he was a young man he had been known as the black sheep of the family and the whole area.

Even in his weakened condition, the fires of hatred and fighting still burned in his eyes. I felt an immediate compassion for him and said, "Howard, I am a Christian, and one of your neighbors, also a Christian, asked me to come see you. We want to love you and be your friend. Is there anything I can do to help you?"

His reply was really unexpected and caught me completely off guard. "Reverend, there sure is. Do you really help people?" I replied, "We sure do." "Well, our roof leaks, will you fix it?"

I thought to myself, "How do I get out of this?" My mind was racing but I came up with no answers, so after praying with Blackie, I departed. I went straight to another neighbor who said he would help with the cost of the materials, if I would do the work. This neighbor was also not a Christian, but we had become friends.

I found myself, on the next couple of days off, roofing Blackie's house. Only one side of the roof was bad, but it was clearly seen from the main street of town, and the neighbor who gave the money was the talkative type, and the whole town saw the new preacher up on the roof fixing the worst sinner in town's roof. It was a providential act of God.

A few days later a local businessman said, "You know, preacher, the town trusts you more in four months than it has all the other preachers in town in the last four years."

Fixing the roof led to many conversations with Anna and Blackie. I studied the scriptures with them. Dolores and Merle, their Christian neighbors, talked with them and in a matter of six months Blackie had made his decision to be a Christian and be baptized. We did not have our own baptistery in our small church so we had to take him to a neighboring town.

On the appointed time one Sunday afternoon, a large crowd of people gathered to see Blackie baptized. He came in his very best 100% wool suit, tie, best shoes, watch and wallet. I said, "Blackie, don't you want to wear our baptismal robe and take off your shoes and take out your wallet?"

His reply was, "No sir, I can't think of a better use for this suit than being baptized in it. My wallet needs conversion just as bad as I do. I'm ready, let's get on with it."

We had to have a couple of men help lower him into the baptistery. The water was very cold! When he came up out of the water his clearly audible words were, "God damn that water was cold." His words were heard by the whole church. He felt so bad about his swearing that he cried and said, "My first words as a Christian were curse words."

I never called Blackie "Blackie" again, nor did his friends. He was "Howard." His wallet was converted and he was a regular contributor to the church until his death about six months later.

Howard had done a real good deed for the young preacher. He had given him the opportunity to gain the confidence of the community. The young preacher had done a good deed for Blackie, "Though his sins were red as scarlet, they were white as snow." He had returned to the name and purity of his youth.

Even though his Christian life was short, his eternity in heaven with God has now continued many years and will for all eternity. What better use of a life could be made than bringing the wanderer again into God's fold?

Ministerial Embarrassments and Baptismal Blunders

One of the most important duties of a minister is that of seeking the lost. It was one of Jesus' main teachings as well as the apostles. It normally comprises a substantial part of the work of the busy man of God. It usually is the source of many blessings as well as a source of a few surprises.

During our Douglas County ministry we were blessed with a variety of people, probably more divergent in background than at any other time during the many years we have been about the Lord's work.

There were people of the full scale of economic brackets. We had the quite rich as well as those in deep poverty. Some were well educated and some could not read and write. Some were from foreign countries.

While out seeking the lost an intimate knowledge of the family workings is often revealed. Several families and people come to mind. Really this is leading somewhere, so don't quit reading until the story is complete.

One of our ladies from the church was a lovely redhead. She was always so proper and dedicated. When I was around her, I always felt I should be as godly as she was.

Every time I would go to the house to call she would greet me gladly and say how happy she was that I had come to call on her and her "unsaved" husband. She wished so badly that he could be interested in the church. Their names were Fran and John.

It was a hot summer day when I came to their door. The door to the house was open, the screen closed. As I approached I could hear loud voices coming from the house. At first I thought it might have been the television turned up loud. Just as it dawned on me what was going on, John, who was facing the door, saw me. His wife was standing with her back to the door.

She was giving him the most awful tongue lashing imaginable. Her words were, "You are the most worthless man alive. You have absolutely no redeeming qualities at all." At this point she threw in some well chosen and angry profanity. I could not believe my ears. Was this the prim and proper "saint" I knew?

I wished I could have slipped off, but he had seen me and to do so would have been cowardly. He began to smile, which made her even more angry. She said, "If you had any character at all you would not just stand there and grin like a depraved sap." Finally, he said in a soft voice, "I do believe if we are to be polite we should invite the preacher in, don't you?"

As she turned to face me, the color drained completely out of her face. She said, "I knew it! I just knew it! One day this was all going to catch up to me, and today it has." She broke into tears and ran away into the bedroom. He and I had the first good talk we had ever had.

It was the beginning of meaningful communication with him, and in a short time John was a Christian. Fran finally came to real repentance in her life, and she became a much more tangible Christian. The uneasiness that I had felt around her was gone. She was not putting on airs, but acknowledging her own struggle and failures as she grew in her Christian life.

The Andreesons

Not too far from Fran and John lived Swen and Goldie Andreeson. They were hard-working Scandinavian people who owned a construction company. Their lives had been complicated by alcohol. "We drink just beer," they would say. "We only drink just beer." They had tried several things to solve the problem and were finally ready to let the Lord Jesus do His work in them. She, more than he, was struggling with alcoholism.

After weeks of teaching they came to believe in Christ and had agreed that on Sunday they would come to make their public confession and be baptized.

My practice at the time was to take people's confessions of faith in the baptistery just prior to their baptisms. The women would dress on one side, the men on the other.

On this Sunday morning the church was full to the front pew. Swen was baptized first. Everything went normally with him. Several other men and a child or two were baptized before it was Fran's turn. When she came into the water I smelled the strong odor of alcohol ("just beer"). What to do was unclear, so I proceeded.

Her apprehensions at being baptized in front of the people had led to stress. This stress led to a beer. After she drank one, several others followed. The warm church, added nervousness and finally the wait in the dressing room had really put the alcohol to work.

When everything was set I said to her, "Do you believe that Jesus is the Christ, the Son of the living God?" She said, "Yassa," nodding her head vigorously. I then asked, "Do you want Him to be the Lord of your life?" Her reply was, "Uh huhhhu...

She was a large rawboned woman. When I started to lower her under the water she pulled her hands loose from mine and grabbed both sides of the baptistery. Try as I might I could not immerse her.

I got her back on her feet. This time I got an iron grip on her hands and managed to baptize her. With the Lord's help she broke her alcoholism and they both became faithful Christians.

Their faith spread to their children and several of their neighbors. It all began with a family with a drinking problem—"only beer."

Associate Ministers

Associate ministers have sometimes been a source of misdirected events and added excitement. Walter was the master of mispronounced words, and also was rather accident prone with two left hands and feet and a tongue that often got in front of his eye tooth.

The church was experiencing a period of growth with frequent baptisms. Because of Darla being hurt at the river baptism, we had begun to use the baptistery at a neighboring church. This proved very inconvenient, as we had to plan around their services and use. They had few baptisms and the baptistery was often poorly cared for.

Our small church had little money, so I endeavored to build a baptistery. I cut a hole in the wall in the middle of the stage, learned the floor support would not hold enough weight for a baptistery, so I shored up the floor with beams, plumbed in a drain and water using the plumbing from the bathroom in the basement below. What a job this proved to be!

I built the baptistery of waterproof plywood and covered it over with polyester resin and painted it with marine boat paint. It came out pretty nice, but the floor was a bit slick. (To the best of my knowledge, this baptistery is still in use.) But it did lead to a disaster for my associate Walter.

During an evening service he was scheduled to do the baptizing. He had led a lady of considerable girth to Christ. Everything was going pretty well until . . . .

Well, it happened that the baptistery had not been cleaned on schedule and the floor had gotten slick. When he started to lower the heavy-set woman in baptism he lost his footing and they were both baptized.

Walter and she went clear under. There was a great wave of water that splashed out on the floor. They both came up like wounded walruses choking and sputtering.

It was rather hard to maintain the type of decorum for which such a holy moment called. We failed at trying to be really religious and proper, and all laughed right out loud. Walter glowed beet red, but even though the moment was not too dignified all 250-300 pounds of her were a new person in Christ.

This was not as embarrassing as what happened to one of my preacher friends. The preacher from one of the non-immersing churches in town had a stubborn candidate for membership that insisted on being "baptized just like Jesus was." Rather than to lose a possible new member the preacher had agreed to borrow a baptistery for the event.

When he came to the church he had a conversation with the custodian cleaning the church building. The conversation went something like this.

The custodian, "Have you ever immersed anyone before?" The preacher's answer was, "No."

Next he asked, "Are you familiar with the process?" The dignified, and a bit proud, preacher said, "Well, sort of." The custodian said, "Do you want some instruction about what to do?" He replied, "Well, not really, I can figure it out."

The custodian asked next, "You do know how to use the baptismal boots don't you?" His reply was, "Oh yes, I know that much."

All of the items were laid out—baptismal robes, baptismal boots and towels. The custodian went about his cleaning and came back just as the baptism was taking place.

The preacher had put the baptismal boots, intended for the minister, on the candidate for baptism. When he baptized him, the boots filled with water. This caused a suction that made it almost impossible to pull off the boots. The boots were filled with water and it was quite a mess. After turning the man half upside down to drain most of the water out of the boots they got them off.

Fortunately, we have never had anyone drown during baptism. Francine had attended church for several months, rather spasmodically. She seemed under conviction, yet whenever the subject of baptism came up she became very adamant, "1 will never be baptized!"

Finally, after weeks of calling and talking I asked in desperation, "What is it that makes you so unwilling to be baptized? " She finally said, "I just can't hold my breath that long." I replied, "How long?" Her reply was, "Not as long as you preachers pray." Somehow she had missed witnessing the frequent baptisms at the church.

I asked, "What do you mean?" Francine said, "Well, you do say a prayer while you hold the person down don't you?" My response was, "Oh no, of course not. You are only under the water for a second or two."

Francine said, "I thought you had to say a prayer in the name of the Father, the Son and the Holy Ghost." She had been reading the Bible and had misunderstood the Great Commission. When she found this out, she was soon baptized and became a steady Christian.

Esther came to church and would sit in the back row. About every third Sunday she would leave the church crying when it was about time to sing the invitation hymn. When I would go to her home she would not talk about it.

I asked, "Esther, you were crying yesterday in church. Would you like to talk about this problem?" She was a very special lady—attractive, bright, and friendly. Her reply was always the same, "Oh, no, I can never talk about this problem."

I continued to call on her from time to time for the next several months. Her married daughter came to Christ, but not Esther. Finally I went out and pleaded with her to give her life to Christ.

Finally, she began to cry and said, "I am so awful that Jesus would never want me!" I tried to assure her that Jesus did want her. She said, "Not with what I have done with my life. I've been married five times."

My words to her were, "You mean that is all that is wrong? The Bible has a story just about you." I opened her Bible and read to her about the conversion of the lady at the well of Sychar.

She came to Christ that very week. She had a new glow in her face and a lot of sadness that had been there was gone. She had come to know the redeeming Christ.

The rites of the church present times of deep reverence, but also chances for embarrassing blunders. Through it all people's lives are changed as they experience the new birth. It is the greatest satisfaction that a Christian experiences and the minister of the gospel has the blessed opportunity to experience it with them.

What other investment of one's life, not only changes people's eternal destinies, but improves almost every part of their lives? A very wise school teacher once said, "The doctor cares for the body—it is temporary. The teacher trains the mind—that also is temporary outside of Jesus. The minister of the gospel deals with body, mind, and spirit—that is eternal." It is a wise investment of a life.

Mr. VFW

He was a man of dignity and there was the bearing of southern genteelness that was usually present. His name was LeRoy Giraldo. He was a veteran of World War I and had many decorations for bravery. His life was wrapped up in the Veterans of Foreign War. He was at every parade and let everyone know that he firmly supported the military.

I can remember him marching down the street carrying the American flag at every parade or celebration. At these times his predominate problem was usually present. His time in the army was his claim to glory from days long gone by. He was now a very old and the most wrinkled man I had ever seen.

He and his wife's little farm was out East Central about five miles. It was set back from the road about a quarter of a mile, up a long and pothole-filled road. The house sat on a little knoll with a number of large trees in the yard. The oak and fir trees that covered the hill rose up to the sky behind the house. It made a lovely setting. The house had the look of a miniature southern mansion, but was now run down from years of deferred maintenance.

There was a little garage out back and a small barn where the Giraldos kept their one cow, a few goats and some chickens that often escaped from their pen and wandered around the yard.

Mrs. Giraldo kept the house clean and I always felt welcome when I was there. I remember well my very first visit. They gave me a dozen eggs. As they were living on a small pension this was a most generous gift and I accepted it with profuse thanks. To have not accepted the gift would have been offensive to them.

Sister Giraldo was a most devout Christian. Mr. Giraldo did

have some faith in the Lord, but seemed to view church as more social than spiritual. He never made a commitment to Christ because he had a friend that was more important to him than the Lord. Because of this problem with the "friends" (tobacco and alcohol), he would always have to get up between Sunday school and church and go out to "Marlboro Country." That was the place where those addicted to nicotine went to light up before, in between, and after church. He was usually the first to make a break for this spot.

I talked repeatedly with him about his relationship with the Lord. He was basically not interested, but nonetheless, was always present at church and treated me with respect. He often offered kind words, saying, "Reverend, it is nice to have somebody that speaks the King's English in the pulpit," or some such thing.

Having no car, going to church gave him a chance to ride in to town with some neighbors that were Christians, and after church to spend some time with his "friend." He would often stay in town and hitchhike home later in the evening after he had his lengthy encounter with his "friend."

Everyone knew LeRoy and few would have let him walk if they had room for him to ride.

Being a young preacher, I was uncertain about a lot of things, and probably should have been more confrontational with him, for he did have a very serious problem with his friend, the bottle.

He was not usually drunk when he came to church, but there were occasions. Such occasions were a real embarrassment to his dear wife. She would get so embarrassed and try to apologize to everyone that observed LeRoy tottering around the building, talking in everyone's face. On many occasions I felt as though I would like to just disappear because of my embarrassment.

One of my very respected professors from college, a man known for being very outspoken, came to visit his student's church. This was one of the very few times he ever came to visit. He picked one of those Sundays when Mr. Giraldo had risen very early to spend time with his friend.

Just as church was about to begin and he had made his last staggering trip out to Marlboro Country, he came back in reeking of tobacco, but even stronger was the smell of alcohol. It was overpowering. I had so wanted to make a good impression on this respected professor.

Mr. Giraldo came in and sat down in the seat in front of him just as church was about to begin. He turned around with his southern hospitality, modified by alcohol, and said, "Whassh your name? I'm LeRoy Giraldo from the VFW. With the friendliness of one made bold with spirits he leaned right up in the professor's face and continued to talk with slurred voice and bloodshot eyes.

I saw what was happening from where I was seated on the platform and was horrified, wishing that I could slip out the door on the stage. The good impression that I had hoped for was lost. I did the best I could with my sermon and knew that there would be some kind of reprimand from the outspoken teacher.

When the service was over I made my way anxiously to the door. The professor waited till most of the people were gone and then came up to me and said, "You had a right decent sermon today young man, but I'm just not used to sitting in a church that stinks like a pool hall!"

I tried to explain, but he turned and strode off, and I never had a chance to explain about Mr. Giraldo of the VFW. Even though the professor and I remained close friends, corresponding by letter at least monthly for over thirty years, he never again attended a church where I ministered. I guess he was afraid it would smell like a beer tavern.

Yellow Creek

Northwest of Roseburg, Oregon the South Umpqua River joins its larger and more beautiful sister, the North Umpqua. Both are beautiful rivers by the standards most people know, but to the people of Douglas County the north river is much clearer and surrounded by more beautiful scenery. The rivers join near a little rural community appropriately called, Umpqua.

There are few ugly parts of Douglas County, but this area near Umpqua is especially beautiful. The area called Garden Valley breaks away from lush farmland into rugged mountains. Some of the hills are logged off and have been replanted to young fir trees that are growing verdantly.

Other hills are covered with old second growth timber, (Those not familiar with Oregon Douglas fir might think of them as old growth. There is really no "old growth" in Oregon as a fir tree dies at 250-350 years normally.) and some are still covered with what is called old growth fir.

The differing ages of trees produce a slightly different color of green and the end result is a picture of many different hues of green. These productive forest lands are well managed to provide an inexhaustible source of lumber.

Some have worried about the cutting off of the old growth timber. Most everyone agrees that some of the old growth should be preserved, especially those stands of timber along the scenic rivers and highways. People who were not raised in the Cascades, but from desert areas or the great plains, have little comprehension of what timber really is to Oregon.

Most native Oregonians realize that to keep old growth, because it is old growth, is as foolish as keeping ripe corn standing in the field to make the field look better. It is Oregon's crop and when managed properly will never be exhausted.

The beauty of Oregon is only damaged for about five years, if, when it is cut, it is promptly replanted. To keep old growth timber after it is mature is wasteful as it stops growing and begins to deteriorate at maturity.

On this particular day we took highway 138 that runs from the small community where we lived towards a tiny village called Elkton. We followed the highway as it runs along the green waters of the joined Umpqua Rivers and several miles past the little place named Tyee, really only a wide spot in the road, as we traveled toward Elkton.

A small stream, named Yellow Creek, adds its waters to the Umpqua as it enters the river from the east. It is one of those friendly little streams of which there are hundreds in this county. It is just right for the wading trout fisherman.

It can be waded across in many places, yet has many pools that are just right for a wary trout to lurk under overhanging branches or some rock or log.

Yellow Creek was just right for the purpose I had in mind on this day. There were many more exciting places to fish, but it became a favorite for me for one reason—that reason was Doug, my oldest son. He was born liking to fish. From the time he was able to walk we went fishing together.

I remember this day in particular for it was a rather warm summer day. It was not the kind of day that one would hope to be prime for fishing. We started too late and it was too warm. But it was just the kind of day that was best for a father to take his young son out along the creek. We would not be cold and if we fell in no one would be the worse for it.

There were several questions that Doug would always ask whenever we went out. We had not gone five miles from home when he began, "Are we lost yet, Daddy?" He was always worried that I wouldn't know the way home. "Daddy are you sure you can find the way back home? Where exactly are we right now?" I assured him that I knew exactly where we were and could find my way back home.

We drove the 20 or so miles and parked the car along the road. From here on it was hiking only. Doug mounted my shoulders, after all he was only about three. He was chattering and excited, expecting to have a great day. He really did have it pretty good, especially him, being in one of God's especially favored spots, him riding, me carrying the creel, bait, pole, and him.

We were pestered by a blue jay that went ahead of us warning all the fish that there was an intruder. These birds can make an awful racket with their squawking. I finally put Doug down and dispelled our obnoxious companion with a few well aimed rocks. He went off squawking looking for someone else to annoy.

We started on and walked some distance away from the road hoping to get beyond the area that the easy going fishermen would have already fished. I kept a wary eye out for timber rattlers as they were reported to be in the area. After about a mile we settled down to rig the pole and bait the hook. We caught a fish on the first cast. It was nothing to brag about, but it might as well have been a prize steelhead as far as Doug was concerned.

It was a perfect arrangement for the boy, he rode, I fished, when I hooked a fish I would peel him off of my shoulders and he would land the fish. His technique was not very refined. The pole had an automatic reel. He would press the trigger and back away from the stream. The poor fish would be literally dragged out of the water onto the bank if it did not escape.

The satisfaction of seeing him have so much fun far outweighed the delight of landing the fish myself. None of the fish were very large. After several hours we had our limit and began to look for other things that lived in Yellow Creek.

One of his favorites were the little waterdogs. These little salamander type of creatures are brown on the back and orange on the underneath. They are harmless to play with and fun for a little boy, but poison to eat, I'm told.

The other creatures we caught were more dangerous, not life threatening, but nonetheless something of which to be cautious. They were quick and ill-tempered crawdads. With their lobster-like pinchers one had to have quick hands to catch them. It is only safe to catch them right behind their claws.

These two little water creatures are pretty good evidence that the water is not very polluted. When the streams feel the pressure of civilization they soon die out. We felt sure that Yellow Creek was pure.

We had taken a lunch along in the creel, and after a few hours we found a grassy place along the creek where we could eat our sandwiches and enjoy a rest.

In this rugged mountainous area the lower hills are rolling and covered with oak trees. The higher hills are covered with fir, alder, and maples in the draws. Along the creek a variety of other trees grow.

Yellow Creek is special to me because it helped a preacher and his son become fast friends, and helped him to grow into the fine Christian man he is today.

The pressures of the ministry can rob a family of the time they need together. It was at times like these that I had to spend with the children that was an important part of their growing up to be Christian adults. There was a bonding of two spirits together that has remained, and will throughout time and eternity.

Yellow Creek provided the catalyst, a beautiful place, a friendly little creek, a warm sunny day, a mess of fresh trout, but most of all a place alone for a man and his son to learn about each other.

We frequented the place often. We loved it enough that we later began to catch and release the fish we caught there. The fish were not what brought us there. We did need the food, but more important was the shaping of a little boy into a healthy young man with a proper sense of values in life. For there not to have been fish to catch would have hindered our purpose in coming.

Do you have a boy? He needs a mom or dad and a Yellow Creek. It may not be a fishing pole, it may be a bicycle, a kite, a trip to the beach, a boat and lake, swimming, or a trail bike. Want good children? Want your children to be a credit to their family? You had better find yourself a Yellow Creek.

When we returned home, by the time we were back in the car, the little fellow was asleep and I was as happy as a man could be. I was ready to get back to my studies and the work of an active ministry. We would soon begin to talk of going fishing at Yellow Creek again.

Do You Understand What Makes Babies?

Al and Kathryn Fisher were faithful members of the small Douglas County, Oregon church where we had our first ministry. They were very faithful. She was the head nurse at Douglas County Memorial Hospital, and Al was a "high rigger." I will explain in a moment.

Al

We were poor as church mice. At the end of most months, our money was gone, as was our supply of food. Margaret, being a farm girl, knew how to can fruits and vegetables. One year she put up 700 quarts of canned goods. But eating green beans and applesauce can get rather boring after a few days at the end of each month.

Here is where Al Fisher came in. Al was the consummate gardener. His garden was loaded with all sorts of great food—cucumbers, tomatoes, carrots, radishes, and luscious corn. The phone would ring about dinner time and it would be Al. He would say, "Put on the water to boil and get ready to eat; I'm going out to pick corn." Al would show up with corn and a basket of other good and fresh produce from his garden. I doubt he knew just how much we needed these items, but God did and He used His servant Al to send us what we needed.

I mentioned that Al was a "high rigger." Douglas County, Oregon, is the mecca of logging of the huge Douglas fir trees. Al was a logger and his job was most unique. At this time logging in the Cascade Mountains was done with what was calld a "donkey" and high rigging. The donkey was a huge diesel engine with big winches to yard in the logs. Al would find two large fir trees at each extremity of the property to be logged, one by donkey and another across the property, swales and valleys.

Al would then climb these trees, cutting off all the limbs and finally topping the tree about 200 feet above the ground. He would then put up large pulleys and cables that ran in a large circle from the donkey and back. One was used to attach "chokers" to logs and tow the logs, several at a time, from where they were felled back to the donkey where they could be loaded on trucks and hauled to the mill.

The circular cable was set up with what was called a "haul back" to take the giant cable and chokers back to get more logs. This was an exciting thing to watch. One day a huge log got caught between two stumps as I watched and the log broke with a sound like thunder.

When the haul back was used to return the chokers to where the logs were, the haul back would become taut and whip into the air 50–100 feet or more. One day a Christian brother, Wesley, was not careful and the haul back cable came up between his legs and threw him 50 feet in the air. He was seriously broken up, with broken pelvis, hip, and legs. Loggers were hauled to the woods in what was called a "crummy" which best described its looks and condition. As Wes was hauled to the hospital, he told me he preached the best sermon he ever gave to several non-Christian loggers. He was patched up and returned to the woods a few months later. Logging was dangerous, and Al's job as a high rigger was the most dangerous of all.

Kathryn

Kathryn was also a special saint of God. She told me to call whenever we needed some medical advice or help, which we did. After our last child was born, I was surprised to see her waiting around near where I was greeting the people as they left church.

Finally, when everyone but she and Al were gone, she said she needed to have a serious talk with me. She began, "Charles, you are a preacher and you will never make much money, and you just cannot afford to have any more kids. I want you to come over to the hospital to talk with me this week. I want to explain to you what causes babies so you will not have any more." As you can imagine, I was more than a little embarrassed. I told Kathryn that I did not need to come to the hospital, as I had been raised on the farm and knew the source of babies, human or otherwise.

It was people like Al and Kathryn Fisher that helped us through the early lean years of ministry. Whenever they come to mind today, my heart is always warmed and I look forward to renewing our friendship in Heaven. See you, Al and Kathryn.

House Calls

The air was so fresh I took several deep breaths after stepping outside. It had the aroma of sawn logs and the faint smell of smoke from the sawmill's tepee burner nearby.

Off in the distance Mt. Scott rose up to the sky. The rocky bluff that makes its western face was shrouded with lacy wisps of clouds. The morning sun was warm and was dispelling the damp coolness.

Today my ministerial schedule called for me to go visiting some of our members who lived out in the country along the creeks and valleys of Douglas County.

Spring is a special time in western Oregon. There are a multitude of flowers and trees of many colors that grow wild everywhere. Some of the first in the spring to show their glory were the dogwood trees. They seem to bloom when the snow is beginning to melt in the high Cascades and filling the streams with the spring run-off. It is that kind of day when I set off to see the Longbrakes.

Other flowers soon to follow were the trilliums, lady slippers (tiny pink orchid-like flowers), followed by the wild cherry trees, foxgloves and the many other native flowering plants that make the area so beautiful.

This morning as I climbed into my Chevy and headed out East Central I saw several of the church members going about their work. Tex was already at work at the grocery store, Elmer Linn at his secondhand store and Vern at his Union 76 station.

I headed for Nonpareil. Nonpareil wasn't really a town but just a designation on the map. In days gone by it had been an important place when the area was a center of logging.

Adventures of a Young Preacher

The Longbrakes had settled many years before on one of the few remaining homesteads. As I drove this morning I passed a little rural church with its white steeple and graveyard alongside. The road then began to wind its way along Calapooya Creek. The creek was crystal clear, as are most of the creeks in the area. We had often (as already mentioned) used the creek as a place to baptize people.

The road entered the heavier forest and began to wind its way to a place where a side road turned off and snaked its way back through the underbrush along another small creek that ran down from the valley where the Longbrakes' farm was located.

The road was narrow and rutted. In times past it showed signs of having been well cared for. The Longbrakes were now old and unable to maintain the active life that was required to care for their rather large farm.

I came to one of the two gates, parked the car, got out, opened the gate, pulled through, stopped, set the brake, got out and closed the gate. This was not my favorite part of visiting this lovely spot.

The road climbed up the side of a ridge and finally broke over the hill where the farm buildings and house could be seen in the distance. The road dropped down and crossed a culvert. I pulled up under a large maple tree in their yard. Two dogs greeted me, trying to wipe their dirty feet on my trousers.

Mrs. Longbrake came to the door and called them off. As I came to the back porch, which was used as their main entry to the house, we walked past a pitcher pump which had been their water supply in years past before they had a modern well drilled. The house was the typical old farmhouse—large rooms, high ceilings, ancient furniture, pictures on the walls, rocking chairs, braided throw rugs over wooden floors.

One picture remains clear in my memory. It was in a round frame and was of three horses' heads, with nostrils flared. Since then, I have seen similar pictures in many places. It spoke of the era of the Longbrakes.

Arthur Longbrake had been ill for many years after suffering a stroke. Since his illness the farm had fallen into disrepair. The house showed signs of deferred maintenance everywhere.

But one could not enter this home without immediately knowing that it was a very special place. Edna Longbrake was there! Even though this visit was over thirty years ago the memory of this day's impression is still fresh in my mind.

There was the smell of fresh baked bread that was cooling on the kitchen counter. Behind was the smell of the wood burning stove in the living room. The place was clean and homey. Out the front window could be seen the serene and secure little valley, ringed by giant fir trees. The little creek gurgled along down the hill at the edge of the front yard. There was a little footbridge across the stream to the garden.

But the greatest reward was still to come to me as a young preacher. When we sat down in the rocking chairs in the living room I was to discover a lady whom the secular world would call "old," but who was in fact an example of the perfected Christian woman. Here she was in this remote and antiquated place. Yet, she was a jewel of perfected Christian maturity.

Her well-worn Bible lay under a lamp by her chair. There was not a part of it, Old Testament or New, that was not familiar to her. She had not only studied and learned it, but during each of the weekly visits over the next three years she revealed new precious insights into the deeper meaning of the scriptures that she had discovered in her daily studies.

Her specialty was a study of the Lord's Supper. Every passage in both Old and New Testament that related to this subject had been committed to memory. To her the Lord's Supper had become a time of intimate communion with the Lord of Glory. Anger, pride, fear, selfishness, and the other imperfections in human nature had long since been banished from her life.

Arthur certainly would have displayed many of these same Godly traits, but the stroke had left him unable to speak.

As a young man of twenty-four I learned a very important lesson. The society that places too much emphasis on youth and physical beauty, misses out on some of the most magnificent people in life. I had gone there to minister to them; in turn they had ministered to me.

I wish today that I could drive out East Central past the little church and graveyard, along Calapooya creek, through the trees, up the rutted roads and exchange theological ideas with sister Longbrake. I do not know how the little valley would look today. Was it the valley that was so beautiful, or the people who had so long made it their home?

Eloquent Profanity Leads to Praise

I had been told by a church member that as a preacher I could get free golfing at the local golf course so I had stopped by to check. As I entered the club house I heard a man cursing in such an eloquent manner I stood shocked. When he paused I said to him, "You must be brilliant to cuss like that!" He said, "Matter of fact I am brilliant." We will come back to Jerry a bit later.

A few days later as I came out of our little church building to my car, a big black Lincoln pulled up next to my car and a pretty lady put down the power window and said, "Would you baptize me?" I replied, "I am not used to having people approach me in the parking lot and ask to be baptized. Would you come into my office so we can talk about it?" She did and that evening, with her husband and children present she was baptized in our new baptistery at the small church. Her name was Ruth.

A few weeks later her two children, a son and daughter, were baptized. It happened that her husband Jim was the golf pro at the golf course and a brother to Jerry the eloquent curser. I continued to pray for the husband, Jim, and his wife, Ruth, became my volunteer secretary. One evening I was on my knees praying for Jim to give his life to Christ when it struck me I should call Jim and try to talk to him about Christ right now. I called their home and Jim said, "Come on over—we are sitting around eating popcorn and not going to bed for a while."

I went, taught Jim and we all went to the church for a midnight baptismal service. Ruth told me a few days later that I should call on her sister-in-law, Jerry the curser's wife. I did and Peggy and her mother were baptized a few days later.

A few weeks later Jerry and Peggy's daughter Suzie also wanted to be baptized. I made a practice of not baptizing children without their parents' permission. I made an appointment to meet with Peggy, Jerry and Suzie. I found an angry dad who told me this story. He said, "I had Suzie baptized when she was a baby and that is all the baptism she needs or will have!"

He then added that as a young man he had decided to become a Catholic Priest. He entered the training and soon found the profound hypocrisy of the Priests. They were committing all the sins of the world while in public professing to be religious. He said, "I have lost all confidence in religion, you are all a bunch of hypocrites and I have no time for any of you." I was shocked and as a young preacher did not know what to say, but fearfully replied.

"Suzie has found friends and fellowship with many fine and upstanding young people her own age at church. She now has her own personal faith in Jesus Christ and wants to do a good thing in being baptized. Frankly, Jerry, I worry that if you refuse her she may just turn the other way and give her life to sinful and destructive activities. Please consider carefully before forbidding her to do what Jesus has asked of her." With a lot of growling and expressed anger he finally agreed to let her be baptized the following Sunday evening. He said, "Don't expect me to be present as I strongly resent your meddling in my family."

Sunday evening came and the building was darkened and the baptistery was well lit. I entered from one side dressed in a white baptismal clothes and Suzie entered from the other dressed in a white baptismal gown. I was speaking about baptism when I observed the back door of the church open and Jerry slipped in and sat in a seat by the entrance. I gave a short explanation of what was happening and then baptized Suzie. When she came out of the water, Jerry came running down the aisle shouting, "Wait, wait, I want to also give my wicked heart to Jesus and be baptized." It a few minutes I was back in the baptistery with Jerry making the good confession and finding his sins washed away. He was genuinely born again.

A few months later, Jim, Jerry, and I traveled to be with their mother and father, whom we taught, and Jerry baptized his mother and father. He also traveled to Georgia where he taught and baptized his brother and his wife. This is another important story for another time.

The Bakers were all truly born again. Jerry was brilliant with a very high intelligence. He went on to learn Hebrew and Greek and taught an adult Sunday school class for over 25 years and during those years served as an elder in the church.

As I write about these events in the life of a young preacher, many of these folks have now gone on to their rewards—Ruth, Jim, Peggy, her mother, Jerry, his mother and father, and his brother George.

Jerry and I talked a week before he died as an old man full of years and mature in his faith. He was 92. We were the closest of friends all those years. It is another example of how important the ministry is and what a good and wise investment is made by those who give their lives to preaching the gospel of Jesus Christ. Few lives produce more lasting and wonderful benefits for humanity. God had but one boy and made Him a preacher.

It is an example of eloquent profanity being turned to eloquent praise through the love and saving power of Jesus Christ.

Bernard and Benevolence

Most people's names in this book have been changed to save them possible embarrassment. This is not so with Bernard Truba. He and his lovely wife Katheryn deserve to be remembered for teaching our small church lessons in benevolence.

People sometimes complain that they cannot find anything to do for the Lord, but this was not so with Brother Bernard. He saw and felt the need of the hurting people in the church family. He came to me and said he knew the church didn't have any extra money, but he was concerned about a poor family in the church whose roof was leaking. He said, "If we did it right we could raise the money and the men of the church could go put on a new roof."

The need was discreetly mentioned and Bernard furnished small envelopes with a big red heart on them. A few of these were placed in the church pew book holders with the suggestion that if anyone wished to help a brother and sister in need they should place their gift in this and drop it in the offering plate as it was passed. A few days later this needy family awakened to find that the leaking roof had been replaced with a new one. Surprisingly the church general offering remained strong and even grew.

Bernard returned to my office a few weeks later and said, "We are having tough economic times and some of our regular families in our church are behind on their house and car payments. Shouldn't we be concerned?" I said, "Of course we should. What do you suggest?" He said if we took up a red heart envelope offering each time there was a fifth Sunday in a month we might just be able to discreetly help these families from time to time as

Adventures of a Young Preacher

needed. If they have a chronic money handling problem we could assist them financially and also with counseling to help them get control of their money management.

The elders agreed to give it a try and the regular offerings began with each month when there were five Sundays. Several families began to be helped from time to time. One family received five months mortgage assistance. Other families did not lose their car or house when the man was laid off or other families were helped who had tragedy strike. Strangely, several families that were helped gave back the money when they got back on their feet. This fund took on a life of its own and to the best of my recollection was never short of funds again.

Bernard's rules were, the person had to be a faithful participating member of the church and they had to be willing to meet with the two-person benevolence team. This team was made up of Bernard and a member who was a financial planner. They would need to be willing to accept confidential help and also financial advice.

One new Christian family, where the man had been a drunkard, were helped get back on their feet and they became one of the most generous supporters of the church. After this man's baptism he never took another drink or smoke, and years later when he died he left an estate of about one million dollars. His life had been totally turned around because of his conversion and of Bernard's benevolence ministry.

For those several years not one person who was a faithful member of the church went hungry, lost their car, or their house. Word got around and those with needs were helped—a widow, accident victim, or unemployed (but no dead beats!) were helped. Bernard's rule was that only genuine needs were to be met by the fund. This fund grew robustly. Bernard and Kathryn Truba taught us about genuine Christian benevolence. This plan could still be implemented in churches today.

It Was a Winning Season

Douglas County is possibly the most beautiful of any county in all of Oregon, with Crater Lake, Diamond Lake, the Umpqua rivers and Reedsport on the Oregon coast. It was fall and the weather was beautiful, with just a hint of cool in the air, but bright sunshine during the days and cool evenings and nights.

Chuck was a member of our congregation, along with his lovely wife, Carolyn (a registered nurse), and two children, David and Lori. They were faithful church members and Chuck was a high school teacher and the football coach. They were highly respected members and soon to be treasured friends as I began my first ministry after ordination. Yes, I was somewhat intimidated by this successful man and lovely wife in the church.

Add to this that his high school football team was having an undefeated season, wiping out all the competition. Of course I was at every home game cheering them on and especially because Alan Cherry, one of our high school youth group, was one of the star players and also a devoted Christian. Alan came from a fine Christian family of seven children along with his parents, Howard and Jean. The whole family was a blessing to the church. Howard did have strong opinions about most things, but most of the time this was good.

I had gotten closer in friendship to Chuck, since a few weeks before, he had come into my office asking to talk with me. He said, "I have been somewhat deceptive about my faith. You see when I started going with Carolyn she made it clear that she would not marry me unless I was a baptized Christian. I agreed to be baptized and was, but my motivation was not Christ, but

Carolyn. I did not really believe that I needed a savior and that Christ was the answer. So, I took the bath, but did not give my heart to Christ."

He continued, "Over the past few months I have been listening and studying and I have come to a strong faith in Jesus and know I must make Him Lord of my life. Will you baptize me?" Of course I was flabbergasted. The new baptistery was full of water and we soon had taken care of receiving his confession of faith and baptizing him in the name of the Father, Son, and Holy Spirit. This added to our already growing friendship.

I must add that a few weeks later his team won the state football championship for smaller schools in Oregon. I was standing at the goal line when Alan Cherry carried the winning touchdown just 10 inches over the goal just seconds before the game was over. The whole town went crazy with delight and Chuck Halstead and his team were heroes in Douglas County.

Chuck continued to coach football and teach high school until retirement. We remained friends and in contact over the years. He became an elder in a thriving church and had a strong influence for Christ in public school.

He called me tearfully years later and said, "Carolyn and I were sitting in our family room talking and she suddenly slumped over and when I got to her she was dead." He grieved terribly over the loss of his lovely wife and lived on another 17 years.

Yes, he had a winning season and a winning life. His children continue to live out their parents' faith today. A young preacher's life helped not only the Halstead's, but thousands of children in high school who had a godly teacher and through Carolyn, a godly nurse tending the sick. Ministry sure isn't dull!

Making Ladies Beautiful

It is often strange which person in the church ends up with the most impact for Christ. In Douglas County, Oregon, it turned out to be a pretty little lady cosmetologist. Elaine was petite, soft spoken, pretty, and gracious. She displayed the characteristics of a mature Christian.

She had her small beauty parlor down on Central Street in the old section of town. It was typical of these places, with several chairs, wash basins, hair dryers, chairs for those waiting to be served, magazines, and Bibles and some Christian literature.

Elaine was not aggressive in her faith, but was always ready to offer a comforting word, good advice, or to offer a verse of scripture that fit the occasion. Everyone in town knew she was a devoted Christian. Everyone seemed to like her and we grew rapidly to love her.

One of her ministries was to see that the preachers' wives of town looked nice on Sundays and this she did free of charge. Imagine my wife's feeling about having her hair professionally fixed, with regular permanents, when we were so dirt poor. In her own quiet way she had tremendous influence for good in this small logging town.

One Columbus Day we had a terrible storm with hurricane-force winds followed by heavy rainfall. I was out calling in Union Gap (remind me to tell you about that later) when the storm hit. I recall watching the roof blow off of a huge sawmill lumber storage building with the metal sheets being carried over the top of the mountain like pieces of paper. As I drove through the storm back home, things were being destroyed everywhere. My car was buffeted by the wind and rain.

When I got back to the parsonage I found the family safe and the house intact. But the church building was not so fortunate. Part of the roofing had been blown off and the rain had poured in right over my desk where my only Bible was laying open where I had been working on Sunday's sermon. It was a terrible mess, swollen 3–4 times its former size with dirty water stains, ink stains, and the cover ruined and separated. I looked at it in despair. It was my only Bible, the one that had all my class notes written in it from my ministerial training. It was my pulpit Bible.

It was an expensive Bible and I thought "How can I afford another one like it as we hardly have enough money to buy food to eat." What was to be done about the leaking roof right over my desk? Yes, I did know how to do roofing (remember Blackie's house), and soon had singlehandedly got matching roofing and fixed the church building's roof. But what was I to do about my Bible?

On Saturday my wife had her hair fixed and she bore the bad news about my Bible to Elaine. Sunday came and went with my destroyed Bible evidenced to the congregation as I tried to use the pitiful mess to preach from.

When I came to work on Tuesday morning there lying on my desk was a new Bible exactly like my old one, thanks to the thoughtful generosity of Elaine.

I could go on to write about the several members of the body who had their introduction to Christ by having their hair fixed by Elaine, who had also helped them become totally beautiful Christian women. Ladies like Della, Sue, Kathy, and many others who came to Christ and, of course, who also influenced their whole families for Christ. Elaine was one of several reasons why the church had such good years in those early days of a young and inexperienced minister of the Gospel of Christ.

Elaine went to her reward years ago and yes Elaine, we have not forgotten our promise to look you up at the Eastern Gate of Heaven when we arrive. We'll be seeing you soon, Elaine.

Union Gap

Between our small Douglas County town and another small town about three miles to the north was a hollow between two hills called Union Gap. Yes, let your imagination run wild, it was that type of place, something maybe from some southern state's poverty section. There were old derelict cars, rubbish in the yards, run-down houses, dogs and cats wandering around, and one auto repair shop along the road with all sorts of junk stacked around it.

The area looked like it had made no progress getting out of the depression since the years of the 1930s. Probably 100–200 people lived in this Union Gap and this led to my interest in bringing Christ to these needy people. We had little influence there until it was time for Daily Vacation Bible School. Each year we put a lot of effort into the teaching and evangelistic effort of the weekday Bible school.

After the Bible school was over, I would personally call on any new family who had been represented by their children having come to DVBS. This led to me going to the Deshaziers' house up in Union Gap. The children had obviously come from poverty and had eaten hungrily at the DVBS lunch we served for the kids at noon. But I was not prepared for what I found at this house.

Now, why would I talk about such people's misfortune? That is a good question and here is the answer. Jesus loves all people and has a special interest in the poor. He displayed this love and interest when He was here on earth. A real "Christian" church should be a welcoming place for everyone, especially the poor.

The health of a Christian church can be measured in part by how they treat every member, rich or poor.

The words of my maternal grandfather came to mind as I approached the Deshaziers' house. "Poor people have poor ways—that is why they are poor." This place evidenced poor ways. Well, this house was the worst mess I have ever seen. It was such a disaster that I volunteered our ladies group to come help the mother, who was not well, clean up the place. We came with a square nosed shovel, a wheelbarrow, brooms, vacuums and various kinds of cleaning products.

The kitchen was unbelievable. The garbage had been dumped in one corner, with food scraps, left over mush, bones and everything just dumped in the corner until it had rotted a hole through the wall to the studs. The place, several hours later, was left remarkably better than when we arrived. Mrs. Deshazier was truly grateful and promised to attend church when she felt better.

Did the Deshaziers come to Christ? As best I can recall two of the children did attend Sunday school and summer camp and were baptized. I do not recall if there was much of a response from mom and dad.

But there was a lot to be learned here. The Christian ladies entered into this project with good cheer and willing hands. We grew closer as friends as we worked together. We did really clean up the place and offered help with food for these needy people.

The love of Christ was shown to them in tangible ways. Union Gap did not prove an evangelistic bonanza, but word spread throughout the county about the good work of the Christians from the church. Thankfully, from then on, when some lady would say, "I am embarrassed; my place is a mess," I could truthfully say, "Your house a mess? No, your house looks just fine to me."

Unbelievable Power

Spring in Douglas County is special, with crocus popping up out of the ground and yellow daffodils waving in the gentle breeze. In nearby woods the white dogwood trees are in bloom and water runs high in the Umpqua River from the melting snow. The air is fresh and the resurgence of nature makes the rainy winter a foggy memory. It was that sort of day as I headed over to the church office from the nearby parsonage. As usual I ran and jumped the front yard fence as I was feeling the vigor of spring.

I was sitting at my rather decrepit desk where the leaking roof had ruined my Bible, and now sat with my new Bible open trying to decide what I should preach about the following Sunday morning and evening. As a young preacher I was always scraping the bottom of the sermon barrel.

A knock came to my office door and one of our lovely widow ladies from the church poked her head in and said, "Can I come in and talk with you?"

Iva had been widowed some years before and was probably nearing fifty years of age, though I never thought I should ask. She was petite, with dark brown hair carefully coiffed. She was very lovely in appearance and demeanor. She and my wife played the musical instruments for church, she the piano and Margaret the church organ. We were both very fond of her.

She sat silently for a few minutes and then tears began to well up in her eyes and run down her cheeks and drip into her lap. She began to sob and as is common with men, the tears began to melt my intelligence. Finally I felt I needed to say something so said,

"My, Iva, you are really upset today, do you think you can tell me why?"

After a bit she got her tears under control and said, "I am going to die soon!" I was shocked because she didn't even look sick. I replied, "Oh, Iva, surely you are not about to die—you don't even look ill today!" She said, "I have been to three different medical specialists and each has made the same diagnosis—I have terminal leukemia. One doctor in Roseburg found it, he sent me to Eugene to another doctor and he sent me to a third. Yes, I may look all right but I have been really sick and that is why I have seen the doctors."

She looked at me and asked, "Brother Charles, what am I to do?" I sat dumbfounded; nothing I could recall from my ministerial training or Introduction to Psychology class came to mind. I silently said a prayer in my mind asking the Lord, "What now Lord?" A passage from James 5 came to mind and after shedding some tears with Iva I said, "Could I read a scripture to you?" I got out my Bible and read James 5:13–18 to her: "Is any among you sick? Let him call for the elders of the church, and let them pray over him, anointing him with oil in the name of the Lord, . . . (v14).

Iva asked, "Just how do we go about doing this? I am to check into the hospital in Eugene tomorrow morning to begin treatment." I suggested that she come to the parsonage at 6 p.m. that evening and I would gather a few of the godly men from the church to anoint and pray for her. This was 1964, the same year as son Steven's birth.

She came, sat in a small rocking chair in our living room and I again read the passage from James and then anointed her with olive oil, and we all laid our hands on her and each prayed heartfelt prayers for her healing physically and spiritually.

When we finished praying, Iva smiled and said, "I feel well for the first time in months." As already stated, she was scheduled to go to Eugene to begin her treatments the next morning.

Upon checking into Sacred Heart Hospital she said, "Before you begin treatment on me today you need to run more tests, I do not believe I am still sick."

My wife and I had traveled to Eugene to be with her and when the results came back we were in the room with her. The doctor said, "I have quite a bit of confidence in the three specialists that sent you to me, but they all three really blew it this time. You have a surplus of good healthy blood. You are not sick. You need to go home as you seem perfectly healthy to me."

We went and bought a card to give Iva that showed a picture on the front of a woman wrapped in a sheet with just her head showing and she was blushing bright pink. It said on the front, "I hear you have been to the doctor for a complete physical examination and the doctor says you have something to smile about." When the card was opened it said, "You were on candid camera." We all laughed until we cried.

The end of the story is that Iva was back at the piano the next Sunday morning. She ended up marrying the most eligible bachelor in town and lived on until she was in her mid-nineties. She and our small church rejoiced in the unbelievable power of prayer.

Pray About Everything

The Apostle Paul says, "In everything by prayer and supplication make your requests known to God." Yes, everything! In another place he says, "Pray without ceasing." His advice is just do not quit praying. Make prayer a part of your daily life.

Here are some areas where personal prayers were offered and answered in this small logging town:

1. For the sick.
2. For people's spiritual needs and lives.
3. For troubled marriages.
4. For financial needs.
5. For jobs or work related needs.
6. For educational goals and needs.
7. For children, grandchildren and great-grandchildren.
8. For wisdom.
9. For our country.
10. For the church.

The list could go on almost endlessly. Here are a few examples of incredible answers to prayer in the life of this young preacher in this small church and town.

With us being so poor, paying our bills was sometimes almost impossible. Our only credit card was a Chevron gas card so I could run the car for church business, calling on members, prospective members and the sick in hospitals in surrounding towns. Somehow this card got to its max and I could charge no more. Why I waited so long to pray was in part due to being young and inexperienced in prayer.

Finally in desperation I was on my knees by the bed Saturday night praying that somehow tomorrow I would find a way to pay off this card. It had grown to $669 with a limit of $650. At the time that amount of money seemed and to me was a small fortune.

As church was dismissed the next morning and I greeted people going out the door a very old person put an envelope in my inside suit coat pocket patting my suit coat and saying, "Do not look at that till you get home. I got a raise in pay and want to share it with you."

When I got home and opened the envelope it was a check made out to him for $675 and signed over to me. Say whatever you like about this, there can be no other explanation than that God heard this poor young preacher's humble prayer.

* * * * *

She came into church looking at me and tears began to form in her eyes. She said, "I lost my job on Friday and if I do not have a job my ex-husband will get custody of my 10-year-old daughter. He is a total loser and drunk. What am I to do?"

One does not have to close their eyes to pray, nor talk in sanctimonious tones either. I addressed Shirley in a normal voice and said to her, "Just look at me with your eyes open while I lay my hand on your shoulder and pray for you." She did as I requested and this was the prayer as best I remember it. "Dear Lord, Shirley has a most difficult life and is trying hard to be a good Christian mother. She needs work badly. In your wise providence will you give her a better job by 10 a.m. tomorrow morning? Amen!" She went on into church as other members passed by shaking my hand.

The next Sunday she came back again with tears in her eyes. Her words to me were, "I got a great job this past Monday morning and am now supervising other employees at my new job." Try to tell her that God doesn't answer prayer and she will laugh at you.

* * * * *

Henry came into church and said on his way past me, "I have been diagnosed with incurable prostate cancer and been given just a few months to live." I shared his pain as I thought of his lovely wife and two children still at home. I said, "Henry, would you be willing to let a couple of the elders pray over you after church is dismissed this morning?" He replied, "Yes, I would like that."

After church three of us gathered to my small office and we anointed Henry with olive oil, making a cross on his forehead and saying, "We pray for you in the name of the Father, Son, and Holy Ghost." We each laid hands on him and prayed the prayer of James 5. Henry not only got well, but is still alive to this day and in good health.

* * * * *

Experience has taught me that none of us pray enough. Pray with anyone who expresses a need, worry, problem, loss, or trial. You do not have to be sanctimonious or change the tone of your voice or close your eyes. In a normal voice you can pray for someone in the checkout line at the store or with the teller at the bank. It can be at a restaurant or in a private place. In everything by prayer and supplications let your requests be made known to God.

There is no promise that every prayer will be answered the way we ask it. If all prayers were answered the world would soon be over populated as few would ever die. Sometimes our prayers are ill-advised or selfish. If answered they would harm us or others. Prayers need to be addressed to God "In Jesus' name." This means Jesus needs to be willing to sign his name on the back of our prayer check. We recognize this fact when we pray in His name.

But Jesus' words ring true, "You have not because you ask not." Just think about it, 98% of those we pray for get well. Thousands or millions of prayers are answered daily. Just think about all the good things God does in our lives. Why not get His active participation in the things you need or want to do. Wow, what a great partner we have in Jesus Christ our Lord. Spread faith and blessings wherever you go by praying for and with people.

The young preacher found his life daily used to glorify God and bless the lives of people in the small town and around Douglas County, Oregon. Just where could his life have been more wisely invested than in ministry for Christ?

Yes, God had one son and made Him a preacher. It is certainly true that not everyone can be a preacher, nor should they be, but a lot more should and they will praise God forever for how useful their lives will become.

Chief Crumly Gives Advice

I was just coming out the front door of the church building when a police car drove up and Chief Crumly got out. His first words to me were, "I don't know why a strong young man like you wastes his life being a preacher." I had mixed emotions about his comment, as I was at first relieved he wasn't bearing sad news about some member of the church, or that I had broken some law and he was there to give me a ticket or arrest me. But I was also embarrassed that he thought I was wasting my life.

He said, "There is another matter I want to talk to you about." He began exhorting me about not training kids to be thieves. He explained that when we leave the building unlocked and there were things of value left inside it teaches children to steal. He said, "I followed two boys into the building the other night and they went right to the small world globe that is used to collect birthday offerings from people on their birthdays." He explained these two boys went right to the globe and had taken the change out of it. He said, "Please don't leave the building unlocked nor leave anything of value, especially money, lying around." I thanked him for his advice and asked if I could explain a couple of things to him.

The building is left unlocked for two reasons. One is so that people with problems can come in and pray in a quiet and holy place. The other reason we leave it unlocked is that occasionally someone comes by that has no place to stay for the night and they are welcome to come in overnight where there is a warm place with a clean bathroom and sink.

"About my wasting my time as a preacher, could I offer my reasoning?" He paused and looked at me rather skeptically. I asked, "Do you not believe in education?" Then I continued, "The church provides excellent educational opportunities for the people of the community and no one is taxed to pay for the facilities or the teachers. The church stands the bill."

"What do we teach? Well, for a few examples, we teach children the 10 Commandments. We teach people to obey the laws and to respect the police. We teach children to obey their parents. We teach the Bible. We help people build self-esteem as they learn God has created them and Jesus loves them. We also provide free counseling for troubled marriages, or for people with emotional or financial problems. We often provide free food for the poor. We help people in times of death. We help people begin their homes in marriage. But best of all, we help people learn about Jesus who will grant them eternal life. We are the only place in town that shows people how to get out of the grave alive."

"Chief Crumly, this just may be the most important work in this town. Take away us preachers and churches and our civilization will begin to fall apart. Your job is really important and we thank you for it, but I suspect my work is also important, possibly the most important profession in our small town. I believe that Jesus, churches, and families are the glue that holds Douglas County and America together."

He returned to his cruiser, got in and drove thoughtfully and slowly down Central Street, and I went in and took the coins out of the small world globe and advised the Sunday school superintendent to no longer leave money in it.

The Brothers

I knew they were coming before I heard their steps or voices—the smell preceded them by twenty paces. Of course my first impression has stuck with me almost like it was yesterday. Their smell could best be described as "musty."

One of their friend described their appearance as "crusty." They were musty/crusty. They usually dressed in suits and ties, but they were from two or three generations past and they had never been washed, cleaned or pressed. Their shirts, in the distant past, had been white. Their ties were spattered with food from the past ten years of wear.

Their clothes served them well, as the same clothes were used, whether in the barn milking or at a church dinner social. Always, the smell got there first. In church the people with clear sinuses would sit at the far opposite part of the church building. Being the preacher had its benefits as I was always at the front of the building. They sat about three-quarters back on the east side.

Arthur was the oldest by three years. Marvin was easily distinguished by his very shaggy mustache that was always long enough to be filled with the food that was filtered through or around it in eating. Other things were often enmeshed in it that should remain unmentioned. Yes, this is gross, but true.

The brothers had lived at home with their elderly parents to care for them until they had died a few years before. The farm was rather large with an old farm house and large barn.

When I called at their home I was never permitted to enter. I tried to find an excuse to get in but they always had a skillful way of directing me to the barn. I tried to peek in the windows, but I couldn't see through the jungle of tall weeds and overgrown bushes.

Somehow whenever I would come the brothers would meet me in the driveway and escort me again to the barn where we would have our visit. I even asked to go to the house, but the subject was always skillfully changed to another subject.

Marvin would say, "Oh, I want to show you our antique plow." Or, "Did you know we had a new calf?" I learned from the neighbors that no one was permitted into their house—well, almost no one. I'll tell about that a bit later.

One would imagine that they would be rather outcasts at the church, but that would not take into consideration how real Christians act. The brothers were part of the church family. We might all joke about them and with them, but everyone from youngest to oldest loved them. They were legends in their own time. Due to the spiritual maturity of the people in the church everyone was accepted in love. The love was genuine.

Church potluck dinners did pose a logistical problem. The brothers always came. They always brought food. It was food they had prepared themselves. Not once, that I can remember, was much of it eaten. But we regulars got there early and kept a wary eye peeled to see what the brothers brought. This meant that everyone in-the-know was there early! Maybe every church needs a set of brothers.

Their car was a part of the legend. It was a Ford sedan with a three-speed transmission and overdrive. It had a big motor and they were often heard to brag how much power it had and how fast it would take off.

At the county men's meeting the church bus would not start due to a dead battery. The driver, brother Harley, was looking for someone with a chain and pickup to tow the bus. Marvin said proudly, "Our Ford will tow it and I have a chain in the car if I can just find it."

You see, the car was so loaded with antiques, odds and ends, and junk that there was barely enough room for Arthur to get in on the driver's side and Marvin to get in on the passenger's side. Arthur always drove. Otherwise the car was full to the ceiling, including the trunk.

Marvin said to me one day, "That sure is a good Ford, but it has one weakness; we had new springs and shocks put on it all the way around but it still will not go on the grease rack at the service station." I thought to myself, a lesser car would not have carried the weight they had put in it.

Marvin finally found the chain and the car was hooked up to the bus. Arthur and Marvin got in and the motor roared. The bus was parked in a gravel parking lot next to the church. When Arthur let out the clutch the dust began to roll and the gravel began spattering all over the front of the bus, some making sparks as it pinged off of the metal. I stood looking on in amazement. I had driven my own car and was a spectator for this event.

Harley said, "My first worry was that they wouldn't get us rolling." That was quickly forgotten as he said, "My next worry was how fast they would tow us. When the bus was started they kept going faster and faster." Pretty soon the bus was weaving back and forth and Harley had to apply the brakes and haul the straining Ford to a smoking stop.

Marvin was proud as punch as we stopped and he came back to the bus, hitching up his pants and tucking in his shirt and saying. "See, I've been tellin' ya how good that Ford is." We all had to agree.

News spreads fast in a small community and I was sad to hear that Marvin and Arthur had been robbed. They collected antiques and especially antique American coins. They were numismatists. They always had a quantity of old coins in the Ford and it was anyone's guess how much they had at home until now.

I called on the telephone immediately to find out what had happened. They were not home. I didn't have to wait long to hear the story. They came to the parsonage.

When they pulled up in front of the house my wife saw them first. We had just purchased a very lovely new couch and chairs for the living room. The couch was a pale off-white with a flower print on it. She said to me, "Whatever you do, take them to the kitchen to talk. Don't let them sit on my new furniture."

I was now the one that needed to direct traffic like they did with me whenever I visited their house. But I didn't have a barn to take them to, or a new calf to show them. Arthur's first words were when he got in the door was, "What a pretty new couch, I'm sure you won't mind if we sit on it." What do you say?

They began telling the story. They had been home fairly early in the morning when two men came to the door of the house. When they answered the door one of the men pulled a gun, and the two forced their way into the house.

He said, while holding his gun on them, "We know you have a stash of old coins here and we want it all. If you don't give it to us we will not be responsible for the consequences."

Marvin got out an old coffee can full of coins and gave it to them. The men were not fooled and demanded more. The brothers tried to talk their way out of this, but it angered the thieves. They were not interested in the plow or the calf, diversionary tactics just would not work, no matter how skillfully employed.

They made both brothers completely undress. Off came the old coats, spattered ties, musty shirts, shoes, rank underwear and shorts. One of the robbers brought out his pocket knife and began to threaten surgery on Arthur's very personal private property. This broke loose a quantity more of old coins. All in all Marvin said they got several thousand dollars at face value of their old coins.

When they were satisfied that they had all of it they took the brothers to their car, tied them up and hauled them out in the country and dumped them out of the car, still naked.

Marvin tried to explain how they felt, "You know we didn't give them our best coins. They got a lot, but not the best stuff." I asked, "But weren't you endangering your brother's anatomy?"

He went on, "It was awful, Can you image how cold we got? Can you imagine going up to a house where there were people we didn't know, naked?"

Arthur added, "I hope the Lord will forgive us being so immodest. Wouldn't you know it, a lady answered the door. She sure was nice. At first she sure looked shocked, but she ran and got some blankets for us to be wrapped in."

The thieves were never caught.

A few weeks later tragedy struck again. I received a call that the brothers were involved in a wreck. As they were traveling to a flea market a car had failed to stop at a stop sign and hit the Ford. It had totaled the Ford and put both brothers in the hospital. It was the one time I saw them in a nearly clean condition, but yet the faint odor persisted.

While we were visiting, Marvin spoke up and said, "Two things bother me most about this wreck. Where will we get another car like our Ford? And, how can I replace my best suit?"

I said to him, "Marvin, your suit must have been forty years old." He replied, "Well, I don't know; I have had it for several years, but I bought it at the bargain day at the Salvation Army. It cost me twenty-five cents. But I really liked it and I know I can't replace it. They just don't make clothes like that anymore." My reply was, "Well, I suppose you will have a hard time finding an antique suit like that one."

Marvin did buy some new clothes. He came into church one morning a few weeks later as proud as punch. He walked right up to me and asked, "How do you like my new bow tie?"

I had a hard time stifling a loud laugh. The mirth walled up in me and was trying to burst out my eyes. I put on my most sober, religious face. He began to explain. "I went to the big city and looked all over town. You know they just don't sell bow ties anymore. I looked everywhere."

What he was wearing was a black satin bow tie designed to be worn with a very formal tuxedo. It had an elastic band to go around under the collar with a hook in the back to fasten it. It was about three times as big as most bow ties. He had on one of his musty old suits with a very mildewed shirt that had at one time been white. The tie was not fastened under the collar, but put around his neck about two inches above his collar. He had not shaved for about a week to ten days, but he had on a fancy bow tie. He explained, "I appreciate the man over at Penny's. He suggested that I go over where they rent clothes and maybe they would sell me one. Wanted it so bad that I paid twenty dollars for it. Don't you think it looks good?" I said, "I must say, it is a good-looking tie."

The brothers were very bright. I too, was a coin collector. They looked over my collection one day when they came to make a social call. Several years later they still remembered exactly what coins I had and what ones I needed to fill out my type set. They could still remember what years my coins were.

What part did the brothers have in the church? I believe they were a great help in teaching us to love others that are a little different from ourselves. In many churches, where faith is weak, the brothers would have been treated with rejection. But because the people in this church loved the Lord they had learned to love those who were different.

In the meantime Arthur has died. Marvin has been really lonely. I have wondered how he is doing and have prayed for him. When I thought about Arthur's death, I have wondered if God had an antique white robe for him when he got to the pearly gates.

Sisters Cut from a Similar Cloth

This story comes many years later in our ministry, but fits here alongside that of the brothers.

It is often said that "lightening doesn't strike in the same place twice." Or, "No two people are exactly alike." Yet the two little maiden ladies were the female counterpart to the brothers.

They too had stayed home to care for their aged mother and father just like the brothers had. They had given up jobs of one sort or another that they had worked at when they were younger, or at least that was the way they told it. I have no reason to believe otherwise.

They did love their parents with an unselfish love, or was it that they felt they might inherit the ranch that their parents owned when they died. It was most likely love of parents that kept them home.

The first I ever saw of them, or should I say heard of them, was one morning when I was working away in my office. I heard this very unusual sound, "Twang, whaap, twang, whaaap, twang, whaaap." It grew louder until it began to slow and stopped with a mighty, "twang, whaap" right outside the office.

I jumped up to look out the window and saw this Ford extended cab, four-door pickup. It was a frightful sight. The red paint was seriously oxidized. The pickup bed was loaded with wet and rotting hay, old hoses, three spare tires and wheels all flat and worn through to the cord. The inside of the pickup was loaded with miscellaneous items till there was hardly room for Martha and Mary to get in.

Adventures of a Young Preacher

Next, I heard them asking my secretary if they could talk with Brother Crane. I always had an open door policy—that is I would talk with anyone who had a need unless I was counseling or in the final stages of sermon preparation or prayer.

They were ushered into my office. The first thing I remember about them was the very same "musty-crusty" odor that was peculiar to the brothers. Both looked like they were very anxious about something, so I asked, "How may I be of help?"

They said, "We have been told that you people here at the church help those in trouble. Is that right?"

I replied, "Yes, we do try to be genuine Christians and help when we can."

This brought a flood of talk as they both began to talk at once. Martha said, "We are just plain out of food at home and our folks are old and we have to take care of them, and thus we can't work . . . "

Mary, broke in, "I guess you could hear our truck coming up the road. We are just up against it. The battery (I could hear it still running outside) is dead and we don't know how we will get it started again. The tire is shot and all of our spares are flat. We can't leave our old parents out in the country without food and transportation."

They told a tale of woe about family members who wouldn't help and church people that didn't want them around.

I suggested that we call a friend at the service station to see if he could begin work on the truck. He came with his tools and soon found that the battery was good but the cable was bad.

The poor front tire had lost about two feet of tread and it had successfully beat out the lining of the fender and was now working on the fender. He replaced the two front tires giving them one rather poor spare.

We took them to the grocery store and bought them the kind of groceries that they needed to get them through till the folks' next pension check came.

This began a long and interesting relationship with the sisters.

Of course they and their parents were in church the following Sunday and continued faithfully in attendance as long as I ministered there.

This created the same sort of problems that we had with the brothers. The circulation in our church building was such that there was no place that one could sit and not get the benefit of the rancid smell of unwashed bodies and clothes. There were overtones of smells from the barnyard, the dogs, cows, and pigs. It was a rather potent blend of malodorous fragrances.

It soon came to a head with one of our fastidious ladies in the church. She came fuming into my office, "Something has to be done about those people. The smell nearly makes me sick. If you don't do something about it, I'm afraid we are going to begin to lose members."

I suggested that they attend the earlier service, but she quickly pointed out to me, "But they attend morning and evening and so do we."

I promised that I would do something about it. I made a trip out to their place. It was one of those cold February days when it was spitting snow, and there was a raw wind.

I pulled down the long driveway as far as I dared in my car. When the mud and puddles looked impossible I got out and walked the rest of the distance to their gate, some one to two hundred yards from their house.

The house was surrounded with an overgrowth of brush that had at one time probably been shrubs. The yard was filled with rusting machinery, old boxes, fence posts, wire, and miscellaneous items that might have at one time been of use around a farm.

I had not heard the dogs bark, but somehow Martha and Mary beat me to the gate.

They said, "We are so happy to have you come visit, Brother Crane." Martha, being the quicker talker said, "We would love to have you come in today, but the folks aren't really up to company, so if you don't mind we can just talk right here in the lane."

I tried to screw up my courage to tell them the purpose of my visit, but everything seemed wrong to broach the subject, and I was beginning to shiver. I asked if we could join hands and pray for the folks and left.

This led to days of apprehension. How was I to discuss personal hygiene with two ladies, approximately 15 years my senior?

I brought it up in our weekly staff meetings and one of the good brothers, Dwayne McMurdie, said cheerfully, "I'll be glad to go talk with them about this." He earned my deep gratitude.

He found on his visit that he was met at the gate. It was still cold and raining and he insisted that they invite him in. They said, "We are embarrassed, the place is really a mess. You see, our well has been broken and we have been bringing water from the creek in buckets."

He found that two big sheep dogs and three cats slept in the very closet where the sisters hung their clothes. He cheerfully brought up the subject of body odor and that it was really offensive to some who were not used to it. We made arrangements for the well to be repaired and they did show a remarkable improvement in odor and cleanliness.

One morning as they were going home from church a drunken driver ran a stop sign hitting their old Ford truck and throwing them both out in the ditch. Fortunately, neither was killed, but this meant that Martha had to walk with a cane ever after. It added to their already desperate situation.

Mother's health began to deteriorate seriously and they felt it best to move to town for the remainder of the winter. In a few weeks she died.

I was called in the middle of the night and quickly went to their home. They were truly in grief over the loss of their mother. It was especially sad for their father, Arthur.

He was an old western gentleman. He wore his cowboy hat and boots, and western cut clothes. In past days he had been a man of dignity and modest wealth. He had lived so long, being unable to work, that he had lived up what he had owned.

I was surprised by the funeral, as the church had continued to help them with food and expenses. The casket was magnificent. They arrived at the funeral in two big Cadillac coaches. The funeral procession was led by two uniformed police on motorcycles. It was one of the fanciest funerals I had performed in several years. Only one thing was lacking, an honorarium for the preacher.

I hadn't expected anything and would have returned it if it had been offered. It should have been a clue to what had really happened.

About six months later the mortician called and asked if he could buy my lunch. At lunch he brought up the subject of the expensive funeral that he had for the Bates family. He asked, "Is there some way that you can help me collect the $5,600 they spent on the funeral?"

I assured him that there was not a ghost of a chance of them paying it and that I was sure that the church benevolence fund could not be tapped for it. He said, "Oh well, I guess I will just have to write it off as a bad debt."

After Mother's death, the family moved back out to the ranch. About a year later Dad began to fail in health and they moved back to a rental in town.

They continued to be faithful to the Lord's house in attendance. They were missing several Sundays, and I didn't have time to stop by the house. I sent one of the callers and they reported that Arthur was ill and unable to come to church.

I hadn't seen any of them around town and began to feel a bit apprehensive. I made a stop at the little house where they were staying. I thought I smelled a rather peculiar odor. At first I thought it might be the two big dogs and three cats. I asked, "How is Dad, I haven't seen much of him lately?" They were rather noncommittal. I said, "Is he in the hospital?" Martha was silent, Mary, the more talkative one, finally said, "No."

I next asked, "Is he staying with your brother?" Mary again replied, "No."

Adventures of a Young Preacher

I said next, "Is he here?" Martha began to cry. "Oh yes, yes he is, we are so upset, we just don't know what to do."

"What is the problem?" I asked.

Mary looked down at the floor for a while without a word. Martha continued to sob.

Finally, Mary looked up at me with tears running down her face and said, "Dad is in bed in the bedroom. He has been dead for five days."

Now I knew what I had smelled.

I asked, "Why haven't you called the mortician?" Again there was silence. Mary finally said, "Well, we haven't paid a dollar on mother's funeral yet. How can we call them?"

I still feel a bit guilty about my answer. I offered, "Well that isn't the only mortician in town you know."

They brightened immediately. Martha ran and got the phone book and found the competitor's phone number. I suggested that before she called, I have a prayer with them as I had to leave.

Sure enough, Falkin Mortuary called me in the morning asking if I would be willing to have a service for Arthur. I agreed that I would be glad to help.

I was not surprised when it turned out to again be one of those elaborate services like they had for Mother. About six months later, I was again invited for a lunch. I was asked, "Is there any way you can help us collect for the funeral?" I said there was no chance.

Since I had been called to testify in court in the settlement of the estate, Martha and Mary did get the farm. It is again being farmed and they are making some semblance of a living.

The church does so much in benevolent work in most communities. This work is of a confidential nature and is seldom even heard about except by a very few who are in the decision making process.

At the time this is being written in the last three weeks about $1,000 in cash has been given out to needy church members or members in the community. Three families have been helped with large grocery orders. One widow's car has been repaired, another's rent paid.

It is one of the great satisfactions of ministry that every week gives an opportunity to minister to the needs of some worthy person although sometimes having a good nose is a hindrance.

Broken Body, Mended Spirit

Our little community was rural, as I have already indicated. This meant that it had no hospital. Our hospital was about thirteen miles away in a larger city.

This area of Douglas County, Oregon is beautiful most all year long with its giant Douglas fir trees, great oaks and beautiful rivers. The Umpqua River is always a delight to behold. The main industry is logging. That is another story.

In the church was a wonderful older lady. She was head nurse at the hospital in the neighboring city. She was rather a matter of fact sort of person who was not embarrassed to talk about anything, especially her opinions. She often let the young preacher in on her wisdom, and I really appreciated it, for it was just that—wisdom.

One Sunday morning after the announcement was made that my wife was expecting again, she waited by the door till everyone had gone out.

Finally her chance came and she said, "Now, preacher, if you have not discovered what causes babies yet, you come on over to the hospital and I will explain it to you. Ministers cannot afford large families because their pay is usually small. You must not let this happen again.

A few weeks later I received a call from her early in the morning. The event about which she called was headlined in the morning newspaper. Two college students from Humboldt State College were traveling to a skiing competition at Mt. Hood, Oregon. They had stopped to help a lady whose car was stalled. There was heavy fog.

When the fog settles in, driving can be very dangerous. I have used a flashlight out the door at night to follow the road, shining it out of the open window at the ground at the side of the car.

While the young man was working under the hood of the stalled car a drunken driver rear-ended the car at an estimated speed of seventy miles an hour. The young man was thrown through the air and bounced off of a metal light pole along the side of the freeway. He was terribly injured. It was about this young man that Kathryn called.

He was an athlete in the prime condition of life. Now he was lying broken and hovering between life and death. As she suggested, I went to visit with him.

My words to him were, "Hello David. I'm Charles, minister from the church where the head nurse attends. She has asked that I stop in and pray for you. Don't try to talk. I'll come back when you are stronger. I just wanted to pray with you." The whole church and county prayed for David.

When David was stronger he began to talk with me. His first words were, "I don't believe in God, I'm an agnostic. I've been studying science and evolution and it has rather eliminated any place for God in my thinking.

I did not argue with him, but went in to visit with him every other day for the duration of his six-month stay in the hospital.

We soon were talking about the Lord. He asked many questions. I answered them the best a young preacher could, often having to do research for an answer. We both learned a lot.

I was deeply disappointed when I went to visit one morning and found he was not there. Oh yes, I was glad he was out of the hospital, but he seemed on the verge of becoming a Christian.

I went to inquire where he had gone and found that he had been flown by ambulance plane to a hospital near his home in southern California. I saw no more of David for nine months.

One Sunday morning just after beginning church services a young man came in the back door of the church building, walked down the aisle steadied by a cane. He came slowly and laboriously down the aisle about half way and was seated.

It took a few minutes for me to figure out who this was, as he was not dressed in hospital clothes with tubes and instruments attached to him.

At the conclusion of the service, when the invitation hymn was sung, he made his way painfully down the aisle to accept Christ and be baptized. He asked to say a few words. This is what he said.

"About fifteen months ago, while trying to help a lady in distress, I was nearly killed as a drunken driver hit the rear of the car I was leaning under the hood to work on. I was thrown over fifty feet through the air and bounced off of a light pole. For days I lay near death. Your minister came regularly to visit. I thought I was an agnostic. It seemed to fit when I was strong and healthy, but it gave me no answers when I was faced with death. It was at this time when my body was broken that my spirit was mended. I wanted to come back here to Douglas County, Oregon to receive true life where I nearly lost my life."

Every eye in the church was wet as David came to know Christ as Lord of his life. An article was carried in the local newspaper telling of his conversion to Christ.

Time passed. David graduated from Humbolt State College. He went on to Yale and graduated with high honors. He is now a husband and father of a fine Christian family. It was one of those cases where the reward was one that money could never buy. It was the best use that could have possibly been made of my life.

It was another case of a broken body that led to a mended soul.

Marrying Sam

There was a most charming lady in this small church. Her name was Reva Bennet. She was middle aged, fascinating, and loved by all who knew her.

She was a public school psychologist. She was the type of person that in times past gave our public school their impact for good and their credibility with the large mass of people. She was a very special person.

She was a great encouragement to a young preacher; the kind of person who had kind words to say after a rather awkward below average sermon. Her husband, Bennie, was also a unique person—quiet, wise about people, and one you could count on to always be the same.

Reva said one day, "Brother Charles, how would you like to come up to the high school and teach a class for me on marriage?

I replied, "What do you want me to teach about marriage?" "Well, the legal, emotional, and religious aspects of preparation for marriage. I have been worried about these young people that have no background in religion and family that are getting married. Their marriages won't last long I fear."

The challenge was accepted. So each year I spent about four days in the high school psychology class talking about marriage. Since I was just barely older than the students I had instant rapport with them. This led to my being "Marrying Sam" in the community for the duration of my ministry there.

Weddings have a peculiar way of fulfilling Murphy's Law— "What may go wrong will go wrong." Such was the case with the Huelshoffs and Blanchfields. She was the shy, small bride, and as with all brides, beautiful. Her father was large and awkward. He was really nervous about his part in the wedding.

This was long before I became aware how nervous the wedding party can be at a time like this when, possibly for the very first time in their life they have to get up in public and say something. Since then I have learned several techniques to put them at ease.

I came to the point of asking for permission for the bride to be married and asked, "Who gives this woman to be married to this man?" Her father got up, cleared his throat and blurted out, "1 do, her husband."

A subdued snicker went through the crowd. His friends were unmerciful to him at the reception. One said, "I sure would like to get rid of my wife, but I wouldn't give her away in public and in church."

Ring bearers and flower girls can be a special area of interest. One little fellow felt he wasn't getting enough attention from the groom. He decided to remedy the condition and right away. So, during the vows, bit the groom on the leg.

These are minor problems in comparison to what happened at the Mumbower-Prescott wedding. Beware of the person in the wedding party who is suffering from a case of nerves. Especially the one who needs some tonic to get through.

One such case was with the best man, Rex Topper. The thought of the crowd was too much for him and he came smelling of liquor. This is the situation that a minister fears most. Who knows just what will happen.

On this occasion, Rex decided at the last minute he had to go out for a smoke. His words were, "I'll be right back. I must have some fresh air and a smoke." He disappeared from the waiting room about five minutes before the wedding was to begin.

Unbeknownst to us, when he went out the side door of the church the wind slammed the door shut behind him and locked. When it was time to return he couldn't get back inside, so went to the opposite side of the church building looking for an open door to get in and found a door that was open. He saw the stairs up to the baptistery dressing room, and he thought, good, I'll go up the stairs and across and down the stairs on the other side to where the men were awaiting entry.

What he hadn't realized was that there was a full baptistery in between him and the waiting room at the bottom of the other staircase. He thought, I'm in luck, the janitor has been cleaning the stained glass window and has left a plank across the baptistery.

As he started across, the plank, nerves and alcohol took over and he slipped and fell into the baptistery going clear under, tuxedo and all. The curtain was closed and the audience could only hear the gasp and splash and thrashing around as he was untimely baptized.

He was thoroughly wet and thoroughly sober. He again made the trip to the lawn. This time to squish the water from his tuxedo. Needless to say, after the wedding there was a big wet spot on the carpet where the double soused best man had stood.

You've Got My Full Cooperation

Weddings provide a special opportunity for the wisdom of children to be made known. This did not happen in our own church building but in another. As the wedding was planned and the wedding party gathered it became apparent that this was going to be the social occasion of the season or decade. Dad, a prosperous businessman, was showing the community how much he really loved his only child—an adopted one.

The most elaborate church of the community had been chosen. The wedding party came with bride and groom dressed in white; the rest of the wedding party was in all colors of the rainbow. It was one of those weddings where nearly thirty people were participating on the platform in one way or another.

The minister was especially nervous because every dignitary from the area was present, as well as a large contingent from the families of the bride and groom. Everything went off well. Ring bearer and flower girl behaved flawlessly to all casual observations.

When the recessional was played, the wedding party went down the aisle to the beautiful reception area, decorated more elaborately than anyone could remember. The minister and mother of the bride heaved a big sigh of relief. They had made it without a hitch.

The guests were gathering to greet the newlyweds and all was quiet for just a moment as the receiving line was posed for a picture when little Jody, nephew of the bride—the ring bearer—piped up in a loud six-year-old voice. "Pastor, during the wedding I really needed to go to the toilet bad, but I knew you didn't want me to run out, so I just did it in my pants.

With blushing mother and bride, the rest of the wedding party and audience roared with delighted laughter.

For ministers, weddings represent a lot of work. Most will take parts of six or more days of their time. There is the rehearsal, premarital counseling and then the wedding and reception. It is a time of beauty and the minister finds real joy in having a key role in establishment of families. Remember to express your thanks to the minister that helps your family at this important time. A generous honorarium would be thoughtful.

A Few Rough Edges

He was one of the first to welcome us to our new ministry. He came in as friendly and warm as a long-lost member of the family. It did bring a warm glow to our hearts to have expressions of love and cooperation expressed. But there was something that left me uneasy. In fact I was pretty sure that he was going to help me grow in the godly grace of patience.

It may have been the three days growth of stubble on the chin, or the automobile that looked like it had never been washed—later I learned it hadn't. It may have been that he left his wife and two children sitting in the sun in the car for forty-five minutes while we chatted in the shade.

We were soon to learn that Walter had a few rough edges. He was a part-time bee keeper. One day while driving with his wife and small children in his Volkswagen bug he came across a swarm of honey bees.

He stopped, collected the swarm of bees inside his car along with his wife and children. Of course every window had to be rolled up tight so that no bees would be lost.

Can you imagine everyone's consternation and unbelief to see him come into town with bees swarming everywhere around upon his wife, children and the windows of the car? He could hardly see to drive. This produced in us a profound appreciation for his wife's godly patience.

Not long afterward Walter came into the office with one of his many hats in hand (hats were his hobby). He nervously worked the cowboy hat through his hands and finally came to the point of his visit.

The Good Twins, gospel singers, were at the church performing. They are known for their mellow tones and ability to blend with each other.

Walter finally got to the purpose of his visit. Fingering his hat, he said, "You know, I am a pretty good singer. I have been growing in Christ and want to serve God." He went on, "You know, one of the twins must get sick from time to time. I would be willing to fly anywhere to take their place in their concerts.

His proposition for me was that he wanted me to contact them to make this sacrificial arrangement for him. He said, "My wife and I have talked it over. Even though I would have to lay off work it would be worth the sacrifice to be a great singer. These are fine men and I want to help in their ministry."

He could carry a tune—a simple one that is—and then not with the quality to qualify him for a regular place in the church choir. It took some skillful talking, but I finally convinced him that he should make the phone call as I am sure they would need to ask some questions.

No doubt about it, Walter's heart was in the right place. It was only a few months later that he was back in the office. This time with another hat—it was more of a sombrero.

After fidgeting around some he finally came to the point. As he looked me in the eye, with his head kind of turned sideways, he said, "You know, I would make a really great soul winner! I've been prayin' about it and have decided that is where God wants me. I want to start callin' with ya."

The preacher that doesn't want people to go calling is three-quarters dead, or probably liberal, or too conservative, but somehow, again, I had feelings of apprehension about this offer.

We set the time to begin. He came in dirty jeans that looked like he had just finished overhauling a car in them. I learned later that it was a pickup he had been working on in them, not a car, but it was motor work.

He had on his work boots that had been greased for water proofing and then left to collect dirt for months. We got off on the call. I desperately tried to select people to visit that would understand, or that might not be home.

That evening as we returned I suggested that we stop for a soft drink. I hesitatingly suggested, "Walter, I think we did pretty good this evening, but there is one matter that needs a little change. When we call we are representatives of the Lord. I believe that personal hygiene is very important. Do you understand?"

He replied, "Well, I guess I didn't clean up much."

The next time we called he came in his suit. He hadn't shaved in several days and he still had the old work boots on. His hair looked like Nebuchadnezzar's of the Old Testament that was described as "eagle feathers." He smelled as if he had not bathed for weeks.

Again, who to call on? It was a big problem.

So, after our calls, we stopped for another soft drink. I explained in detail, "We are working for the greatest institution that has ever been on the face of the earth—the church of the Lord. We should look better than if we represented General Motors or Dupont.

I went on to explain that he should bathe, shave and get really fixed up. I am not sure what discouraged him. Maybe it was all this cleanliness. He did not last as a personal evangelist.

He did return to volunteer. This time God had called him to be assistant Sunday school superintendent. This time he came with a welder's beanie cap. He perceived the assistant's job as one in which it was his responsibility to round up every child that was about the church who was not where he thought they ought to be, and take them by the ear to their class.

One parent reported that he had hit their child over the head with his Bible. Another said he had dragged theirs back to class by the arm. Again, he had to be gently removed from his place of service.

After a sermon on hospitality he had another calling of the Lord. I do not recall what hat this called for—maybe a chef's hat. The first family was blessed with a tremendous helping of homemade chili. There were copious amounts remaining after dinner and they were placed in the freezer.

We were the next to be blessed by his newfound gift—hospitality. He did the cooking in the family. We were asked to be at the house at 2 p.m. on Sunday to enjoy a meal with them.

We arrived just in time for Walter to decide that their kitchen table was too small. With the patio door open he hauled out their kitchen table and began to drag old lumber into the kitchen. The lumber was covered with dirt and weeds. Out came the skill saw, hammer, and tools, and by 3:30 a picnic table was built and the beans were beginning to thaw on the stove.

All the time an electric bug zapper had been at work right outside the patio doors. Over the past months a huge mound of dead bugs had collected under it. We had spent our time trying not to sit around in the sawdust with our Sunday clothes.

Really, the chili beans were pretty good. By four o'clock we were getting quite hungry in spite of the zapped bugs, sawdust and delay. Hospitality continued the next week with another family being invited to participate in what had now been refrozen twice.

One of the elders and his wife were invited to the fourth participation in chili hospitality. They all got food poisoning.

Walter decided that hospitality wasn't his calling.

Where did Walter fit in? Everyone, especially I, wondered if he had a talent to use for the Lord.

Finally he volunteered for sound man, to control the public address system. There he found just the right place where he could serve. He took the job very seriously and proved as faithful as anyone could be. There he became indispensable, and he was important to the well-being of every church service.

I can still see him making last minute adjustments to the microphones, waiting till most everyone was in place, then adjusting the equipment to get it just right so everyone could see that he was doing his job.

During all of this there was a metamorphosis taking place in Walter. He cleaned up, he learned to be more diplomatic, and he learned to be more careful of food.

But most of all, he grew as a Christian. Those of us around him learned to love and admire someone who had lots of good in them, even though they had a few rough edges.

The Ravens of God

The early years of our ministry were not marked with great financial rewards or success in reaching great numbers for Christ. The truth was that after graduating from college and taking a church, our income decreased by 80%. The part-time college job had paid much more than I would earn in the ministry for many years to come.

It was a step of faith to quit the good job with decent pay, insurance, retirement, and a vehicle to drive for one that had very little of anything to offer but challenge and people everywhere who needed the Lord.

The financial realities of life have often discouraged those beginning in ministry. On paper, or with a calculator there was no way to figure out how to make the inadequate supply of money go around.

But in actual practice there was much to learn about faith during those lean years in ministry. Some of our very warmest memories relate to how God supplied our needs through His people.

The Bible tells how Elijah was fed by the ravens while he was by the brook Cherith. Not all such miracles are confined to the pages of the Bible.

The beginning minister can experience similar lessons on faith. God will, in miraculous ways, supply the needs of those who seek to serve Him and will trust. Many heartwarming occasions, when God supplied our needs, come to mind.

Our pay in those years was $70 a week. We had a car payment of $67, and sometimes our gasoline bill was over $100 a month.

After we had paid our tithe of $35 we were left with $78 a month for food, clothing, medical needs, telephone, etc. There was never a month when the money would go around, yet God did supply.

During these years Elaine Erickson was probably the most faithful raven of God. She would come by with gifts of money or food. It was always in the most gentle and encouraging way. We were never made to feel like charity cases, but genuinely loved. When we had nothing, she would show up to share with us some special blessing she had received.

As stated elsewhere, on one occasion my Bible was destroyed by a storm that blew off a part of the church roof right over my desk. My only Bible was ruined. The insurance company paid me quickly for the destroyed Bible, but the money had to be used for food. I still had no Bible. Elaine purchased me a new Bible. It was used as my preaching Bible for the next ten years.

Mr. and Mrs. Clifford Johnson milked two cows. They would bring milk to our home. We would find two gallons of nice fresh, clean, whole milk on the front porch in the mornings. Otherwise we often would not have had any milk for the children. Was not this God sending his ravens. Both Brother and Sister Johnson have long since passed on to glory, but their good works are yet remembered.

During those years we canned every fruit or vegetable that was brought to us. Very little spoiled. One summer this represented over 700 quarts of good food that we canned that came to us as gifts. True, applesauce gets a little tiring after being interchanged with pears and green beans with nothing else to eat for a few days. It was healthful and we did not suffer from being overweight.

On other occasions, when the situation was getting desperate, Tex Johnson, who owned a local grocery store, would bring by a food order that came from some unknown source—probably him. Later we discovered that it was an expression of the Johnsons' love and sensitivity to God's leading in their lives. They too were ravens.

Al and Kathryn Fisher always raised a big garden. Al would

come by with big sacks of fresh vegetables. He would call and say, "Put on the hot water, I am going out to pick corn." These dear folk would bring gifts and at the most appropriate moments. Did they realize that they were ravens?

Hunting in those days supplied our major source of meat. God used nearly miraculous means to see that we got our allotted supply of venison.

Chuck Haistead was my usual hunting partner. One Sunday morning at the close of church he said, "Why don't we throw in our old clothes and guns and after the area singspiration at Yoncalla we can cut back over the hill and make a little run down through the woods and see if we can find a buck." Hunting had been a little slow and I had begun to pray for assistance.

So when the singspiration was over at 3:45 we were in the church rest room putting on our hunting clothes. We took the road back over the hill and parked the car near a large grove of oak trees.

The deer eat the acorns when the weather turns cold and rainy. It was one of those days when the rain was dripping from the trees and we could slip soundlessly down through the trees and brush.

We were hardly out of the car when I heard Chuck shoot. He had gotten a nice acorn-fattened three point buck. We were back with the deer hanging up in the garage and at church by 6:30 p.m.

A few days later one of the ladies of the church called and asked, "Do you hunt?" I replied anxiously, "Yes." She said, "Two big bucks have been coming in with our cows each evening when I bring them in to milk."

"You probably could get them if you would come out this evening." This was especially important because I had been so consumed by the church duties that I wasn't having time to get the necessary meat in the freezer.

Chuck Haistead and I were there at 5 p.m. Sure enough the two nice bucks were there, and another was added to the locker.

The next season, the night before hunting season opened, the phone rang at about 10 p.m. One of the hunters in the church said, "How would you like to help me get a deer tonight?" I said, "But it is night and the season doesn't open until tomorrow."

He said, "Don't worry, I'll be right over if we can use your car." In a few minutes he came and said, "Let's go and I will explain." The man was of the highest character so I played along. We climbed into the car—he had no gun, but did have a flashlight, knife and some plastic.

The story began to unfold. When returning from a football game the bus had struck a trophy buck in the road killing it. He had gotten out and cut its throat, making all the team stay on the bus.

He continued with the story, "You know that deer that are run over are just left to rot along the roads. It would be a sin to let such a nice piece of meat spoil when our families are in need."

By this time we were at the scene of the accident, or should I say blessing, or crime? The huge buck was down between the two lanes of the freeway. He got out with flashlight in hand and had me drive 100 yards down the road saying, "I'll signal you when it is time to back up and load."

When cars came along he would lay flat on the ground. Finally he signaled and I backed up and the deer was loaded. Young and idealistic, we did not realize the seriousness of our malfeasance. All we thought was, our families needed food and the deer were left to rot along the road side.

As we started for home I said to my friend, "How are we going to explain that the deer does not have a bullet hole in it?" He said, "Say, we do have a problem don't we?"

"Hmmm, we must shoot it."

After a few moments of thought he said, "Why couldn't we take it out behind your house in the little barn. The sound of the sawmill will cover up the sound of the shot."

As we started towards the little barn in the dark, I began to worry again.

I said, "Won't the bullet go clear through the deer at that close range and maybe hit someone's house?"

He said, "Well, we could cut most of the head off the bullet couldn't we?" We did.

I said, "Where are we going to shoot it?" His calm reply with a sly grin, "right between the eyes of course." He had a plan forming in his fertile mind.

So the deer was shot directly between the eyes. The next morning by 10 a.m. it was hanging in his carport. It was the biggest trophy buck of the season that was killed by anyone in our town. Again, God's (??) "raven" had been at work filling our freezers with food.

Years later, the horns of this trophy buck still hung on this friend's living room wall to remind us of how God had supplied our needs and how that night we had salvaged a nice supply of prime venison for food during the winter months. Among the many in-season events remain this out-of-season one.

Douglas county remains a place for good hunting. There are deer, elk, bear and an occasional mountain lion. Fishing also supplied a good part of our diet as we enjoyed the bounty of nature for those willing to tap that resource.

During these lean years we had one large hospital bill. We had no insurance. When it came time to pay the bill money began to come from many different sources. When the money was tabulated there was all but $15 of the total bill. It was only right that we pay part of the bill for our son's pneumonia and stay in the hospital.

These lean years still bless our lives. We are still willing to give our last dollar to help some brother or sister in need knowing that God will supply our needs with His "ravens."

"I Can't Do Much, But I Can Make Money"

I was there to try out to become their preacher. An old man, wrinkled, but with a gentle spirit and warm bright eyes said, "If you come to be our preacher I will become a member and help you in every way I can." At the time I did not think much about the conversation. Later I learned to love this fine and godly man like a second father and he turned out to be one of my best teachers.

After being installed as the preacher in the small church, he and I became very close friends and he confessed that he wished he could have been a preacher of the gospel. He repeatedly said, "The church is the only thing on earth that has a real future to it." Whenever I needed to travel to preach, teach, or serve God he asked to go with me and we traveled thousands of miles together.

Let's begin at the first chapter of his life. When Ralph was nine years old, his mother and father died of typhoid in Iowa. He had an older brother, 14, but no other known relatives. Since his folks were share croppers, the two boys had to vacate the humble home they had known. He and his brother hitched a ride on a railroad train heading west. Two days later his brother got into a scuffle with a hobo riding the same train. The hobo threw his brother off and the train ran over him and a wheel cut him in two. Ralph had to borrow a shovel to bury his only known relative. He was now on his own and had only finished the third grade in school.

He joined up with a Barnum and Bailey circus troupe where he did odd jobs until he was old enough to take out a homestead in Gooding, Idaho. He told me he planted his first crop without aid of even a hoe or shovel, but used his bare hands to pull the sagebrush and till the soil to plant a small garden to feed himself and his new wife. He worked hard at farming and began to buy old worn out tractors and farm machinery and sold parts to farmers with broken equipment.

This he did until he was 54 years old, when he and his wife Mina were invited to a revival meeting in Gooding. They accepted Christ and he became convicted about his smoking. He said to me, "One day I took my carton of Camel cigarettes and put them on the fireplace mantle and said, 'God deliver me from this filthy habit.'" A year later Mina said to him, "Ralph, can I burn those cigarettes?" Which she received permission to do.

Soon after, they decided to move to a larger city where they could sell his used car, truck and tractor parts. He sold his Gooding farm and took half of the money and gave it to the Christian Church, took the other half and bought some land and a few weeks later the main highway was run past his new land. He started up his used parts business. He told me, "I had never tithed and probably everything I got was really God's." This was the reason for his generous gift to the church. He credited the change of the highway route to God blessing him for his faithfulness.

He said from then on everything he touched turned to gold. I found out that he was a multi-millionaire. He became such a blessing to this young preacher and church. He often said, "I don't know how to do much, but I do know how to make money."

While traveling with him, he would get out his check book and ask me to write a check to this or that mission work, or for a needy widow, or church project, and he would then sign it and have me give it to the person. These checks were often for multiple thousands of dollars.

Traveling with him provided some of the best education for me. Some of his sayings have blessed me ever since. For example, he often said, "It takes wind to fly a kite." I asked what he meant by this. He explained that a church or business cannot grow without advertising. He said advertising is like wind is to a kite.

Another of his sayings was, "You never make money selling something; if you do not buy it right you cannot make money selling it. Business success is in buying not in selling." Another saying often repeated was, "Work is too hard to do to not have money working for you." He told me how to invest and where one could make money best work. I learned that he had hundreds of thousands of shares of stock from companies all across America. His parts business grew to include new as well as used parts and became the largest truck and auto parts business west of the Mississippi River. It was worth millions. He often said that God gave him a gift of making money so he could give to the Lord's work.

One day while I was talking to his wife, she said her clothes dryer was broken. I asked why she did not call the repair man to fix it. She said, we try to save so we can give more money to missions and the church. I went to my car and got my small tool box and fixed it for her. As I left she gave me a $100 bill. Yes, this money was needed, much like Elijah needed the biscuits brought by the raven.

My church pay was pretty small and we struggled constantly, especially with car expense to call on members, visit nursing homes and hospitals. One night I was distraught because my credit card bill was to the max and they would not let me charge anymore to it and I had no cash for gasoline. I was on my knees asking God to direct me and help supply this need. The next morning at church Ralph put something in my suit pocked, patting me kindly. He said to me, "Don't look at that till you get home." At home I found it was $10 more than my Chevron bill.

Years later he called me one morning and said, "Will you have my funeral?" I said, yes, but you sound pretty healthy. He replied that he was feeling just fine, but liked to have his plans made well in advance. Three days later I received a retainer check for $750 for having his funeral someday. The strange part was that I had borrowed $3,000 to give to an important church project and had trusted God to help me repay it as I did not have resources to pay such a large bill. My first installment was due and God had put it in Ralph Hafer's heart to send me the money just when needed.

His lovely wife, Margaret, grew ill. She had become the matriarch of the church and all of us turned to her in crisis when we needed special help in prayer. I had by then gone on to another ministry states away. Knowing of her illness, I traveled to visit her so I could pray for her. After I prayed for her I asked if she would give me a matriarchal blessing. While I knelt before her she placed her old and feeble hands on my head and prayed a wonderful prayer. When she was through she said to me, "Don't ever worry when you can pray."

The lessons to be learned are that when one serves God you are never alone. When things look darkest is when Jesus brings His light to bear on you and pour out His blessings. Ralph and Margaret Hafer were saints of God who used money as their special tool of ministry for the church. "I can't do much, but I know how to make money and can give it help the Lord's work." (Mini had died years before and Margaret and Ralph had married a few years after her death.)

A minister often is not well paid financially. The lessons learned from Ralph Hafer have blessed our lives and those of the family. "Work is too hard to do to not have money working for you." –Ralph Hafer.

Hoof in Mouth Disease

The preaching minister and his family are often in the public eye. This provides many opportunities to put one's foot in one's mouth. When these occasions arise, efforts to remove the foot often lead on to even more embarrassing explanations.

To take one's self too seriously is a mistake. It is better to laugh with those that are laughing at your misery. If this is possible, the event can become an asset rather than a liability.

My sweet misery began here in Douglas County. These moments applied not only to myself but other members of the family and church staff.

Our daughter was always grown up for her age. One evening at a church ladies meeting she decided to explain her situation as she was growing up. She was in the first grade.

Her words were, "I used to be just a baby. Then I grew and got into kindergarten. Now I'm in public school. The next thing you know I will be a teenager and then I'll be in adulteryhood." Over twenty years later some of the ladies still recall her efforts to talk like a grown up.

One Sunday morning, with the wife sitting in plain sight of the whole congregation, my first words were, "I don't get enough love." After she had glowed like a red light bulb I tried to explain. These efforts seemed so futile the elders got together and decided that maybe I didn't get enough love.

As a group they came by at the close of the morning service and each gave me a big hug and kiss.

We had an older minister serve with the church for a couple of years. He was highly esteemed because of his dedication to the

Adventures of a Young Preacher

Lord and obvious love of God.

It has been said that, "If something goes in one ear and out the other it isn't as bad as if it goes in one ear, is scrambled by the brain and then comes out through the tongue."

Calvin was the master of the mispronounced word. He had a very limited education but was very devoted to the Lord. He was willing and anxious to preach at any time.

Can you imagine our consternation when one Sunday he began his message by saying, "Today I am using a co-text."

On another occasion he gave a lengthy sermon from Jeremiah, chapter 36. Jehudi read Jeremiah's words to Jehoiakim. As Jehudi read the king would take his pen knife and cut off the page and throw it into the brazier. Our dear brother read and referred to the word the whole evening as "brassiere." We wondered if he understood the words he read.

On another occasion he preached a sermon from Acts 17 about Paul's sermon on the Areopagus. The word is properly pronounced Air-e-op-a-gus. He called it the Aero-pay-cuss through the whole sermon. We had visions of Pecos Bill.

Weddings provided another opportunity for getting the wrong words. When it was time to exchange vows, his apparent preoccupation with the fact that the bride was quite heavy set came out.

When he meant to ask, "Do you take this woman to be your lawful wedded wife?" Instead he said, "Do you take this woman to be your awful leaded wife?" The embarrassed snickers of his wife could be heard throughout the rest of the ceremony.

We began to look forward to his sermons wondering what newfound insight of pronunciation would be forthcoming. The end result was good. We still remember his sermons that otherwise might have been readily forgotten.

A public speaker quickly learns to hurry right on past the faux pas of speech that are an inevitable part of being in front of the public so frequently. When you, as preacher, come out with a real hummer, remember it may be the only sermon they remember.

The power in preaching is not the preacher, but the word of God. When the preacher does not take himself too seriously, God can use our weakness to His glory.

The Lennial Reigns

The phone rang urgently. The voice on the other end of the line sounded worried. "It is about Brother Eric. His sister thinks he may be in danger of taking his life.!"

He continued, "I am calling you because I have never faced a problem like this and she wants me to come. I've promised to come and I don't know what to do. Can you come with me?"

By this time it was clear I was talking to one of the men from our church discipleship group, Ben Hatton. He had helped lead Eric to Christ and was working with him in discipleship. Now he faced a problem beyond his ability.

I must confess that as we hurried to Eric's home my heart was beating faster than normal. When we arrived his married sister met us at the door and began to tell a most bizarre story. She was almost beside herself with fear for her brother.

About this time Eric appeared from the bedroom. He was wide-eyed and looked like he had suffered a severe sunburn. But before we get ahead of the story let's back up a bit.

Eric was first contacted by the church calling group because of the concern of a Christian relative. He had been on drugs for several years and had finally realized the seriousness of his condition and was ready for help.

During the teaching sessions he would arise and go to the kitchen and after running some water would return and again enter into the study.

Several sessions later he said he could tell when we were telling him the truth because he could go take a drink of water and if it tasted good he knew we were telling the truth. If not, we were telling a lie. Fortunately for our teaching the water came from a very pure source and always tasted good.

After weeks of study, Eric accepted Christ and was baptized. He was joined by several other members of the family. He had gotten completely off of drugs and was working hard at his job. Today, though, he looked as frightened as a wild animal cornered by a pack of hounds.

"Eric, you don't look so well today," I said. "What has happened?" He replied, "I can't tell you except only that Jesus is coming in His Lennial Reigns in three days!"

"Can you tell me a little more?" I asked. This seemed to make him even more afraid. We followed him as he paced back and forth from one room to another.

Seeking to find an answer to this perplexity and in an effort to find out why he looked so bad I asked, "Eric, you look so bad today, isn't it possible to tell your preacher what has happened?"

Hesitatingly he began, "I . . . 1 . . . I'm not supposed to talk about it, I'm forbidden."

"You mean you can't tell your preacher?"

"That's right. The messenger said if I told anyone about it I would not become the new Son of Man."

"Eric, I think you had better tell me what has been happening. Certainly God would not forbid you to tell your preacher about something that has you this upset?"

This seemed to open a floodgate, and he said, "A voice spoke to me a few days ago and told me that Jesus was coming back in His Lennial Reigns and that if I would do exactly as I was told I would become the new Son of Man and would rule in the Lennial Reigns. The messenger told me I had to fulfill several things. I was to fast and pray for seven days and then I was to climb to the top of Mount Scott and stay for two days and nights naked."

"I went to the bottom of the hills and parked my car. Just as the voice had told me. I took off all my clothes and climbed up through the brush. It was so cold. There was snow on the ground beginning about half way up the side of the mountain. It was dark so I wasn't too embarrassed. As you know I am strong and used to the out of doors, but I was so cold I thought I would freeze to death. I stayed up there about half of the night until I am sure the Holy Spirit was coming upon me. I could feel the energy just shooting out of my fingers and toes."

"I know I must not be too spiritual yet as I got so cold I just couldn't stay and towards morning I had to come down. I am so afraid that I have refused to do what God has told me and now His Lennial Reigns is about upon us and I am so scared. I know I must go back up the mountain tonight and if I don't I won't be ready for Christ's return, and if I do I am afraid I will freeze to death."

I recalled that the weather report confirmed that Mt. Scott did have a light covering of snow on its upper reaches and the forecast for the night was colder with precipitation.

It was enough to strike fear into anybody. His sunburned appearance wasn't sunburn at all—it was frostbite and chapping from exposure to the cold and wintery weather. Just what should I say to Eric?

I was praying earnestly for God to give the right words. I asked, "Eric, do you listen to Christian radio?" He said, "Yes, I sure do."

I then asked, "Have you been listening to preachers preaching about the Millennium lately?"

"Well, yes."

Then, "Has that worried you some?"

He looked at me and said, "Yeah, it sure has."

"Well, Eric, the Bible nowhere even uses the word millennium. Did you know that?"

He said, "No."

I went on, "Many teach different things about this doctrine. The teachings are conflicting and often not founded on scripture. Eric, the Bible calls Jesus the Son of Man. It is a term not used for the rest of us. Did you say that the voice said you were to become the new Son of Man?"

Adventures of a Young Preacher

Very quietly he said, "That's what it said."

"Eric, the Bible says that our bodies are the temple of the Holy Spirit and that if we destroy the temple of the Holy Spirit God will destroy us (I Corinthians 3:16-17 and 6:19-20). What you have experienced is a voice telling you to endanger your very life."

"Eric, for three reasons I feel sure that the voice you have been hearing is not the voice of God, but of the Devil. God would not have spoken of 'Lennial Reigns.' God would not have told you that you would become the Son of Man. God would not have told you to risk your life by going out in the cold naked for two days and nights. Eric, the voice you have been hearing is not God speaking to you."

"Eric, do you believe that I am a man of God?"

"Yes, Brother Crane, I do."

"Eric do you believe I would mislead you?"

"No, of course not."

"Well, this is what you should do. I want you to go over to the restaurant and get a good warm meal. Do not eat too much or you will be sick."

"From now on don't listen to voices that speak to you and give you messages that are contrary to the teachings of the Bible."

There is a lesson in this for many young people today. Even though Eric had become a Christian his mind was still affected by the damage that was done by drugs. Jesus had changed the direction of his life, but for years he will bear the flashbacks from his time spent on drugs and serving the Devil.

There was a deep sense of satisfaction for Ben Hatton and I as we returned home and later when Eric was married to a fine young lady. He still needed to grow a lot in Christ, but where could one have been more useful than the afternoon of the "Lennial Reigns"?

Brother Fred's Pants

Children are the future of the world, nation and church. As a preacher I have always had a special interest in children. The church needs to make special plans to minister to children.

As a young preacher it soon became apparent that I would do lots of speaking. In our small community I taught about family and marriage at the high school due to the influence of sister Reva Bennett, a member of the church. This meant that I had more weddings than any other preacher in Douglas County.

With preaching morning and evening each Sunday, and teaching an adult class in the morning and a youth class in the evening, I did a lot of talking. By the way, there was also Wednesday night prayer meeting and Bible study. Add to these the weddings and funerals and I was constantly talking. It was not long before I realized I needed to carry breath mints to lubricate my vocal cords and make me more pleasant to talk with.

Scott, a cute red-headed boy, was the first to pick up on the little candies that I carried in my pocket and asked if he could have one. Other children soon clued in to the fact that the preacher had candy in his suit pocket. Before long I was giving out several rolls of Certs each Sunday morning.

These were sugar-free candies, but one mother pointed out that I was shaking hands with lots of people and touching the candies as I peeled them off of the roll. She pointed out this was unsanitary. I heartily agreed that I needed to change my practice.

The very next Sunday I had a bag of Tootsie Rolls and these were a super hit with the children. When church dismissed, there would come a flock of kids. I suggested to the adults that their

Adventures of a Young Preacher

faith was fixed and the children's was not; let me quickly greet the kids and then they could come next.

This particular Sunday an older member, who had been sick in the hospital, came out with his cane and I said to the children, "Let Brother Fred come first to greet me since he has been quite ill." Fred came up and I reached out and shook his hand. As I did so his pants fell off. (He had lost a lot of weight while sick.) They were cheap polyester material and lay around his ankles. The kids and I were about to have a stroke trying to stifle our laughing.

I did not want to butt heads with Fred, so I let him deal with his fallen pants. He chuckled and laboriously managed to get them up and hold on to his cane with one hand and his pants with the other as he walked out of the church lobby.

Many of these children today are still serving the Lord because the church was a place where they were loved, learned their Bibles, and developed faith in Jesus as their Lord and savior. Many of these have gone on to wonderfully productive lives with fine families and children of their own. What would have happened to these children if had not been for a young preacher who cared about them? Some still remind me of my giving them Tootsie Rolls when they were small children.

The Parsonage

The church residence for their minister is often referred to as a parsonage. I suppose the word parsonage came from describing the place where the parson lives. Maybe it is where the parson is aged. There may be some truth to that thought but the blessings far outweigh the negative things. Well, maybe.

The origin of the parsonage must have been somewhere in the medieval past. At least some of the parsonages must have had their origin there. A couple we have lived in were old enough to qualify as historical monuments. One needs a sense of humor about things like that.

The day of the interview for our first church we were given the guided tour of the parsonage. Everything looked pretty good around the house as we were sort of hurried through it. There were so many new things that it didn't really sink in what we were about to experience.

The lady giving my wife and I the guided tour was telling us exactly how the past minister's wife had decorated the house and where their furniture was placed. When we came to the kitchen her little daughter spoke up cheerfully and said, "Oh yes, and this is where she always kept her dirty wash stacked!"

The house had four bedrooms, a living room, one bathroom off of the kitchen, and a tiny laundry room, also off of the kitchen. One bedroom was upstairs and must have been made for little children with very long legs. The steps were two feet high and about five inches wide, while the ceiling of the stairway was very low.

The house was heated by a very ancient wood stove that had the grates and lining burned out of it so that when it was hot the ashes and coals fell out on the floor. It would not hold a fire. This meant that there was never any heat in the night or early mornings. It was also a fire hazard.

The roof of the house needed repair, but this was not much of a problem because it only leaked in the closet where we kept our clothes. Imagine my consternation when arising on Sunday morning to find that my one and only suit and shoes were soaking wet.

The house sat several hundred feet back off of the street next to the church building. It had been years since it had been painted—inside or out. The siding was deeply weathered until it resembled the siding on an old barn. It had hardwood floors in the living room and downstairs bedrooms. These were so rough it was easy to get splinters in one's feet.

Really, we did appreciate the efforts of the people to provide a place for us to live. Yet the poor house had so many deficiencies. The very problems have been the source of many a laugh and of some warm and cold memories for our family.

Since the parsonage belongs to the church, church guests are sort of expected to be welcomed there at any time. Such was the case with Clayton Kent and his lovely wife. They were at the church for our very first evangelistic meeting. Guests have been viewed as more of a blessing than burden and many beautiful people have visited our home because of this system.

Yet my wife and I were somewhat nervous at the thoughts of having such important people as our first ministerial house guests. These were people from another state that were widely known and very special.

The revival was going well. He and I were making plenty of evangelistic calls. One afternoon he requested I drop him off at the house early. He wanted to rest a bit and work on his sermon for the evening. I had some more calls to make on people who might attend the meetings.

Mr. Kent decided to take a bath. My wife was over at the church practicing on the church organ for the evening music. Our children were playing around the church building while she practiced. When she returned to the house she heard our son Doug, who had preceded her to the house, talking with someone in the bathroom. He was about four (there had never been a lock on the bathroom door) . She walked in and said, "Do you always take a bath with the door standing wide open?" expecting to see me in the tub, while in fact it was our respected evangelist. He was stretched out full length in the large tub. She blushed every time she saw him the rest of the week which was frequently.

We moved into this house in mid July. When winter weather set in, a small pond of very stinking green looking water developed in the backyard. This became a concern, so I began to investigate its origin. I checked the septic tank. It appeared fine. It certainly should have been fine.

Next, I crawled under the house. To get to the place where the plumbing was under the house I had to dig a hole under a large beam that ran just above the ground. After I had dug the hole I found a terrible mess. Both the tub and toilet had been draining out on the ground under the house for many years. Just getting to the place to work on it took no small amount of character.

This problem took a lot of work to repair. The pipe from the toilet was offset so that about two-thirds of what went down went on the ground. The tub drain emptied on the ground. Use your imagination as to what this was really like under there.

Over the years we learned that a parsonage could be the source of many sorrows.

A committee of church ladies were often placed in charge of deciding about needed decorations or repairs. Seldom were these repairs performed promptly or professionally. Often the committee could not agree and if they did there was no money to make the repairs or improvements.

Our next parsonage was a very lovely older house. We felt a great sense of relief to be in a much better quality home at last.

One of its lovely characteristics was a winding staircase to the upstairs bedrooms from the front entry. We were certain that we were going to enjoy this home very much.

Exactly one week to the day after moving into the house a repairman was working on the range. The range experienced an electrical short. Someone had put pennies under the fuses. The repair man did not realize the problem until the house was burning all through the attic.

The fire occurred during prayer meeting. The wife and children were at home due to one child being quite ill. When the house caught on fire she came running into the church building, which was next door, in her bathrobe yelling, "Fire, fire!"

My first questions was, "And where are the children?" They were all in bed asleep.

I ran out of the church across the snowy yard, up the winding staircase, in the dark (no electricity as the whole electrical system was now burning) through a smoke filled house, into the two bedrooms finding the children and carrying the two down the stairs. My lungs were bursting by the time I got outside. I then ran back in and got the sick little boy in the downstairs bedroom.

We had just finished putting things in place that day. Now all of our things were carried out through the snow and into the church basement and dumped in one big smoke-reeking heap. We sat and cried, feeling trapped. Nowhere to go, totally dependant on God.

It was 15 degrees outside in the snow. We were in a new state with a congregation of 40 members and homeless. At times like these it would be easy to ask, "Where is God?" Instead we added another to our list of reasons we did not quit the ministry.

During the next months we moved five times before we were finally settled into what was our own home—another parsonage. We lived with another family for over two months. Nine of us in three bedrooms.

After several months a house became available to buy near the church building. The deacons decided to buy the house, but one of the deacon's wife was very upset. She was terribly distressed, "I have not had time to pray about this important decision we are about to make. I need a month to pray about it."

My patience was finally totally exhausted and so I said, "You mean we have been homeless for three months and you haven't gotten around to praying about it yet?" That cleared the air and we soon had a lovely brick home.

Later as we looked back on these events we felt God was wanting to give us a much better place to live. We rejoiced in the new brick home with a double garage, fenced yard and quiet street. We experienced many joys there. We learned that it is through many tribulations that we come to be of real service in the kingdom of God.

Following the fire we lived with one of the families from the church. There were nine in our two families. What appeared to be a real hardship turned into one of the closest friendships we have made over the years.

Tom and Ruth Bender became some of our most treasured friends. One evening Tom volunteered to make banana splits for the whole family. He did a fair job. The next night it was my wife's turn. She learned from him and did even better. The following night it was Ruth's turn. She did even better. Not wanting to be outdone I purchased three gallons of ice cream and made banana splits for everyone in large Tupperware bowls. That called f or a truce and an end to our banana split contest.

Our next experience with parsonages was during seminary days. We moved into an old parsonage that had served as such for nearly 100 years.

An old picture of the house showed it looking much the same as it did when we lived in it. The picture had been taken during morning church. The street was corduroy—that is, lumber and brush laid in the mud. In front of the house were horses and buggies that were lined up where people had left them during church. Over the years it had not been changed or improved. Deferred maintenance was everywhere.

In the center of this large, old, high-ceilinged, two-story house was a massive chimney that ran from the basement up through the roof of the house. This chimney had a very firm foundation and had not settled. The rest of the house that was anchored securely to the chimney had settled. The foundation had rotted down until all of the floors sloped to the outside of the house. Anything dropped or spilled ran to the outside of the house.

One day the kitchen sink plugged. Being an amateur repair man and recognizing how long it took the parsonage committee to act, I took repair into my own hands. The snake did not work to free the clog. Draino also produced no results. The next step was to take the pipe wrench and crawl under the house.

The basement was only under part of the house and was not under the kitchen. Crawling back through the cobwebs of many years to where the pipe came through the floor, I put the wrench on it and gave a gentle twist. The pipe broke off at the floor and also about thirty feet away at the other end where it went out through the foundation of the house. Falling on the ground it broke in three pieces. What had been anticipated as a half hour project turned into an all day one.

The bathroom was in the upstairs right over the downstairs dining room. Because of poor maintenance the toilet had leaked over the years until the floor was rotted away under it. When it was used it would rock back and forth. We often joked, wondering what would happen if some heavy-set person might use it during some Sunday dinner and end up on our dining room table.

The laundry room was in the basement. When we had electrical storms and rain, as we often did, we would lose our electricity. The sump pump would not work, so the basement would fill up with water to the level of eight to twelve inches. This necessitated setting the washer and dryer on cement blocks that were stacked on top of each other. Of course there was no need to fix this problem since one could not wash with no electricity. When the electricity came back on the pump would empty the basement in a couple of hours.

During freezing weather in the winter the water would leak in between the walls and freeze. This made the walls swell and huge icicles formed where the water would seep out between the siding.

We spent very little time complaining about the conditions of the parsonage. We felt God knew our needs and would supply. We did begin to grow more and more weary of the parsonage system.

The fine Christian people in the church recognized the need for the old manse to be replaced. Where would we live for the six to ten months it would take to tear down the old building and build a new one? In this small community there were very few places for sale and none for rent.

A church member offered a little house with 800-900 square feet of space. It became our dwelling while the new parsonage was under construction. It was only partially built and had many unfinished projects.

The agreement with the owner was that we could rent it if we would finish these projects. One of these projects required me to crawl under the house and finish the plumbing that ran through the floor and not to the drains. You guessed it, the house was a lake underneath. I was again crawling around in water and mud, but at least it was not sewer.

While under there I discovered several bare, hot electrical wires that had been run through the floor and not yet connected to anything. Fortunately, I had not made contact with them.

Plans were drawn, money raised, and soon we began to tear down the very old parsonage. The new parsonage was one of the finest homes in which we have ever been privileged to live. It had four bedrooms, a full basement with a fine sump pump, kitchen, living room, formal dining room, family room with fireplace, and most important to me a large double garage with automatic opener, hot and cold water and a drain in the floor. During cold weather I could wash the car in the garage. The people sacrificed a great deal to provide this fine home for us. We were deeply appreciative of it.

When we moved into the new home the decoration committee had not finished their work. One of the ladies, Beth Williams, could not decide what color and quality of drapes should be put on the windows.

For six months we lived in the house without a drape or shade on the windows. Our bedroom was right next to a grocery store parking lot which had a large halogen light that shone in our bedroom window all night. For six months we undressed and dressed in the bathroom, crawling to and from when needing to use it or when in our bedclothes.

Our friends, with whom we had lived two months after the parsonage fire, came for a visit. The wife was incensed at them not providing window coverings.

The committee met for another of their many meetings to discuss what color and quality the drapes should be. After listening for a little while the elder's wife sized up who was so inconsiderate of our needs. She told Beth just how she felt in no uncertain words. Beth ran out of the house in tears. In ten days there were beautiful drapes on the windows.

While we were living in the small interim house, while the parsonage was being built, my wife's mother became very ill with cancer. She needed my wife's help. I was left alone with three children, church, and seminary for four months. I was a full-time student, preacher, mother and father. I was chief cook, bottle washer, launderer, taxi driver, hospital visiter, and general parent.

One Thursday evening the owner of the small house in which we were living, came to the door and said, "I'm sorry to have to tell you this, but I have sold this house and you have to be out so the new people can move in tomorrow." I was too dumbfounded to even reply. I just stood and looked at him, and he turned and walked away.

To my knowledge there was not another vacant house in the town, or maybe county. Knowing this lack of housing I called the prayer chain at the church and asked everyone to be in prayer for our needs.

Within two hours John Gordon, one of the very fine deacons from the church, came to the door and in the most gentle and kind way said he thought he had a solution to our needs. A few months before his aged father had died and left a beautiful old mansion in town vacant. If we didn't mind storing our things in a classroom at the church we could live there. We did for six or eight months.

We went from living in a tiny little house with no room to a gigantic old mansion. In one night I changed from sleeping in our rather poor bed to sleeping in a bed with a canopy over it.

In a few weeks mother died. Again this lovely Christian brother came to our house. He brought with him an unsigned check. He said, "Here is a check for you. Fill in the amount you need to take the whole family out to Oregon to your mother-in-law's funeral."

I asked, "How much did you have in mind?" He said, "About five thousand dollars." That much was not needed, but he did pay about eight hundred dollars of our expense to fly out to be together as a family during this sad time.

What did we learn from these experiences living in other people's houses? We learned that happiness is a one-day-at-a-time thing and has very little to do with the kind of house one lives in. Even though the old parsonage was cold in winter and hot in summer, we had some of the happiest years of our lives there.

We learned that in whatever circumstances we found ourselves we could be happy and were. We learned that no matter how bad the situation—house burning down, house sold out from under us, illness in the family, God was real and met our every need.

I promised my wife that we would never again live in a parsonage. We have encouraged churches everywhere to get away from this archaic system when possible.

Summer Camp and the Crow's Nest

Our ministry in Douglas County, Oregon began the first of July in 1962 and my first duties were to go to three weeks of summer camp at Grove Christian Service Camp above Dorena Lake on the beautiful Row River in Lane County, Oregon. This camp was in the foothills of the Cascade Mountains.

Upon arrival, my first impression was that this camp was paradise or at least just on the edge of it. It was along the beautiful, small Row River, nestled among huge fir trees, with several hundred acres. Hills ascending to the south and the river to the north were the boundaries of the campgrounds. There were lacy vine maple trees among the huge fir trees back along the mountainside along with other beautiful plants and ferns native to this part of Oregon—it was a paradise.

The camp had a fine lodge with kitchen, dining hall and a large meeting/chapel room for services. There were 15-20 cabins along the hill to the south with one cabin farther up the hill and to the west that had earned the name "The Crow's Nest." We will come back to that later.

The daily camp schedule began with the bell ringing to announce it was time to get up and prepare for breakfast. We would line up outside the dining hall, sing a couple of songs, pledge allegiance to the Christian and United States flags, have a short morning devotion, a breakfast prayer, and then eat.

After breakfast on the first morning of camp, the campers were divided into families that would be their small group for the week. Mornings were given to classes on a variety of spiritual subjects and then chapel just before lunch. Chapel had singing and a sermon directed to the age group present. (We had three camps, Junior's, Junior High, and High School.)

Lunch was a rather happy affair with singing, jokes by staff, and a good time in general. Students or staff were picked on and made to sing or tell stories. All of this was done in good humor and fun. When the meal was finished, one of the family groups was chosen to do the dishes.

Afternoons were devoted to having fun. There were fine ball fields, for softball, volley ball, and badminton. The favorite hangout was the swimming hole in the river. It was the most perfect natural river swimming pool in my memory. Being the youngest preacher and also an avid swimmer, I was made the life guard for all three camps and had to rescue those encountering difficulty. We used the buddy system, teaming two people together to watch the other. Swim wear was monitored to ensure modesty.

The Crow's Nest

Being new to Grove Camp, I was finagled into being the cabin dad for the Crow's Nest. I had no idea what that meant until the first night in the cabin. I found that all the "jocks" that were wild, planned to get into this cabin. It was noted as the party place with all sorts of events going on often well into the night.

I learned that the year before when it was time for the daily cabin inspection, which they usually failed, the inspectors found the door of the cabin nailed shut with a sign, "Noah's Ark, behold God hath shut the door." Of course, inside the cabin was a mess.

My plan for the cabin was to teach them good habits of nightly devotion and prayer. The first night we got through this fairly well with me giving a short devotion and my praying for all of them. I explained that the next night I wanted each of them to join in audible praying. Then the lights went out.

That was when the cabin came alive. First, there were all sorts of disgusting sounds, some natural and some contrived. (Use your imagination; yes that was what was going on.) This brought on loud hooting and more disgusting sounds. Then began the crude stories told in disguised voices in the dark.

I was ready for them the second night after learning that one or two of my cabin had raided a girls cabin during the afternoon and taken some of their underwear and night wear and put it up the flag pole. They had sneaked out after I was asleep to hoist these things up the flag pole. It was on display when we came to breakfast. (I did a little research and learned that we had a parent's phone number for each boy in my cabin.)

When the lights went out the second night and the raucous fun began, I turned the lights back on and said, "I see none of you are tired so I have a little project to help burn off some of this excess energy. Get up and put on your pants and follow me." I took them to the chapel and had each pair of two boys pick up one of the old and heavy church pews and made them carry them around the ball field a few times. I said, "When you are ready to sleep we will return to the cabin."

One brave soul said, "I won't do it." I said, "Well, I have your mom and dad's phone number and I guess I will have to go call them to come get you." He said to me "You wouldn't do that would you?" I replied, "I will gladly call as I am used to sleeping at night." A few more rounds around the ball field and we all went to bed and slept.

The next day I prepared for the coming night. I had found two or three fellows in the "Nest" that I felt I could trust and enlisted their help. They had agreed to my plan. I suspected one fellow, the ringleader, to challenge me this night. Sure enough, he did. The fellows did as I had instructed, got up, took this rather scrawny fellow to the river, nearby, and threw him in. I had said, "Be sure to take some towels to dry him off. In a few minutes they were back with one rather drowned and shivering kid. The nest was now secure and quiet for the rest of the week.

By the end of the week, each young man had made significant spiritual progress and the ringleader had been baptized the second time, accepting Christ as his Lord and Master.

The next year many of the boys wanted to be in the "Crane's

Nest." It proved to be a very productive time in the "nest" in helping mature young men in Christ.

Competition

Camp was lots of fun and games, but also carefully planned to bring maximum spiritual growth. For each game of ball there was competition among the families to try to be the winning team. The winning team got more points and each losing team also got fewer points, so each team's points would build, win or lose. This led to fierce competition between the teams to try to earn the winner's prize at the end of the week.

Also points were given to each team for their teammates learning biblical things. They could win points for reciting by memory the books of the Bible in order to their captain. There were lists of important scripture verses that could also be memorized to earn more points. The winning team did so by these memory points more than the ones from the games usually. There were prizes presented in the final chapel for the person who learned the most Bible verses and all of the winning team members. These prizes were nice Bibles. A Bible was given to the person who had learned the most Bible verses and to each member of the winning family team.

Campfire

The highlight of each day usually was campfire. There was a large fire ring with a burning fire. It was the only light. We sang choruses and then had a message from one of the ministers. This was an exceptionally impactful time and the goal was to be sure every camper went home a Christian and if they needed to be baptized they were at camp or at their home church on Sunday.

Sometimes the message was replaced by an enactment of some Bible event or story. The following story was not done at Grove Camp but at another camp by one of my friends with a much more vivid imagination than any of us at Grove Camp.

Elijah and the Prophets of Baal

This evening at campfire they were to have Elijah appear. He came with a turban and robe (actually a blanket) for covering. An altar was built with large rocks upon which a stack of wood was carefully laid. Someone had gone into town and bought a couple of stuffed animals to serve as sacrifices. All was laid in readiness for the Prophets of Baal to come dance, howl, shout, and cut themselves, trying to bring down fire from heaven to prove their god Baal was real. All of this was to no avail.

Now it was time for Elijah to entreat Jehovah God to send down fire from heaven. Elijah (actually one of the preachers) had three boys bring cans of "water" which were in reality "gasoline" and pour it over the altar. Up the steep hill behind the campfire circle was a hidden person who had strung a wire from a tree and fastened it to a rock on the altar. He had put a roll of toilet paper on the wire that had been soaked in kerosene. When Elijah called down fire from heaven he lit the roll of TP and sent it hurtling down the wire.

There were a couple of unfortunate things. First, the boys getting the gasoline took all of the caretaker's gasoline, about 15 gallons. The next was that this was a hot evening and the fumes from the gasoline had wafted up, the gas had run down into the trench, and from the trench ran down the slope into the river. When the burning TP got close to the altar there was a mighty roar and explosion knocked Elijah down and set his robe and turban on fire.

The animals were soon burned up, the trench filled with gasoline was burning and the fire went down to the river and even the river was on fire. (They did not re-enact the killing of the Prophets of Baal and Asherah.) The campers learned a lesson they still talk about years later, God answers by fire when His prophets call. It is not smart to mess around with God's prophet.

The Value of Christian Camping

These three weeks in July were exhausting. At the next church men's meeting back in Douglas County one of the deacons suggested that since I had already had three weeks of camping I should forgo my vacation time. My response was, "Next year I will gladly let you take your vacation to take my place at the three weeks of camp. I will spend my time with my wife and children."

These weeks were some of the most fruitful of the ministry for this young and inexperienced preacher. Most of the campers were led to Christ if they had not already been. Many went on to form Christian families, to become Sunday school teachers, deacons, elders, and preachers.

The names of a few of the campers who became preachers come to mind—Mike Whitford, Jon Steadman, Alan Cherry and Russ Isom. There were others that do not presently come to mind. Looking back over the years, these may have been the most productive weeks of ministry.

Very few people, in any field of work, have offered a more useful and satisfying contribution to humanity than helping young people get their lives on the right track while still in school. Not only were hundreds blessed, but summer camps became the recruiting place for the next generation of preachers. These were some of the blessed in-season times for sure.

Camp Christian Colorado

As a young preacher I was invited to speak at another camp near Glenwood Springs, Colorado. It was in a remote canyon with a beautiful large creek flowing through the middle of camp. The routine was similar to Grove Camp and I had been invited to be the campfire speaker. (There were about 150–170 high school campers in attendance.)

The campers were preachers and students from the Western Slope churches. There were cabins, chapel, and cafeteria like most camps have. I especially remember one sermon I preached at campfire that week. I entitled it *I Was Saved By Good Looks*. The three divisions of the message were: 1. A good look at myself. 2. A good look at the Bible. 3. A good look at Jesus. This particular campfire has stuck in my memory because when I asked who would like to give their lives to Jesus, there were 45 high schoolers who came to be baptized.

We did have some fun at this camp, and especially at lunch. Another preacher and I contrived to entertain the campers at lunch. This preacher was Mervin Johnson, who was noted for his fun loving sense of humor.

At the first lunch we had what was called the world's greatest spitting demonstration. He was the spitter and I was the catcher. This happened over the heads of the campers at the dining tables. He would spit special shots; the loop d' loop, the curve, the splatter, the sinus flux, the round the room, each with supposed spitting and I was to catch it in a gallon can. When I caught the spit I would thump the bottom of the can. (I had this can about 1/3 full of hot water.) Someone yelled out, "He is not spitting at all, only faking it." At that point I flung the hot water over the crowd and one's mind doesn't work fast enough to realize it isn't spit but just clean warm water. A moment of pandemonium broke out with everyone trying to wipe spit off of themselves.

The next day at the same time just as lunch was coming to a close Mervin came out and begin to yell, "The Viper Man is coming, look out—the Viper Man is coming, looking back over his shoulder as he came through the cafeteria." I was then to come in from the outside with another can of warm water, with white towels over my shoulder and a squeegee in one hand and a can of hot water in the other hand. I was saying in a loud voice, "I'm the Wiper Man." When I had walked through I turned and flung the warm water over the crowd.

The next day led to a real disaster. We had conspired to have an Indian rain dance this day. Mervin and I came in robed in blankets, with gallon cans and big spoons to thump on the cans while we had a rain dance. After a bit someone yelled out, "It's not going to rain." That called for us to spray our warm water from our cans over the crowd.

The disaster followed about three hours later when there was a gigantic cloud burst up the canyon above camp and shortly water was raging through the camp and over the bridge three feet deep. It didn't wash away the camp, but we were all terrified for an hour or two. It was decreed that Mervin and I were never again to do another rain dance at Camp Christian.

From Camp Christian came the next generation of preachers and leaders for the churches of Colorado and the Intermountain West. How could a person better invest their lives than to impact thousands of people lives for time and eternity?

Think You Would Like to Travel?

I didn't sleep much that night. My mind was running all over the Middle East. It had been caused by a minister who came to our area men's meeting with his slides of the lands of the Bible. He had pictures of Petra, Jerusalem, Jericho, Egypt and other places that seemed so remote that I had never had even the faintest hope of being able to visit them.

From then on traveling to the lands of the Bible never entirely left my mind. It was one of those impossible goals, but all things are possible with God.

The next day I was talking about visiting the lands of the Bible. My wife said, "Don't think of going and leaving me home. If you go, I go!" I replied, "That makes it just doubly impossible. For one to go is beyond my comprehension, for two to go makes it beyond reach."

Well, God made our dream come true, and since then we have gone on many world tours and to places we didn't even dream of, because we didn't even know they existed. On each of these trips we felt a deeper and deeper appreciation for the opportunities that come to a minister of the gospel for travel.

Yet, the dream of travel started while we were there in beautiful Douglas County, Oregon. There have been so many exciting things happen, where should I begin. Why don't you come with me on some of these excursions to various exotic places.

Zimbabwe

The flights from Portland, Oregon to London were uneventful to the extent of being almost boring. We traveled over the polar route, much of which was covered with clouds. We had been up at 5:30 a.m. after not sleeping much. We could not help ourselves—we slept on the overnight flight.

We had a layover of about eight hours in London's Gatwick airport. This meant we really didn't have time enough to run into London as we did not know we would have this long. Our flight was delayed about three hours from the time we were scheduled to depart.

Finally we heard our flight called for loading and we got our first glimpse of the airplane that would be carrying us to southern Africa. It was a Boeing 707. I recalled that they had been produced in the 1955 to 1957 era. They always had been a good airplane so we did not worry.

When the plane was ready for departure we were pleased that it was only about one-quarter filled. We would have a lot of room to move about on what was to be about a twelve-hour flight. We had hardly started down the runway before we were in the air and soon the pilot was throttling back.

Soon after we had crossed the English Channel the plane began to descend and we landed in a short while at the airport in Frankfurt, Germany.

We taxied up to the terminal and alongside of three huge stacks of goods that would have filled three large semi-trucks. Soon there were men swarming all around the airplane and they began to load the airplane. I thought to myself, certainly only one of those giant piles of things is going to be loaded on this airplane.

For the next three and one-half hours they loaded and offloaded the merchandise, motors, potatoes, washing machines, and huge crates of unknown contents. The worker stood back and scratched their heads, got out their calculators, loaded and offloaded until all three stacks of goods were on the plane. I began to worry.

Then passengers began to load. People, most of whom were of African origin in appearance, came aboard with arms full of luggage. Things were stowed overhead, under the seats, and finally in the aisles. My fears turned to serious prayers. But before long it appeared that the airplane was loaded to the point that there was no more room to put anything inside.

The doors were closed and the motors began to hum. We began to taxi down the runway. Although the runways were in perfect condition, as we came to the cracks in the cement we could feel the plane thud heavily and shudder.

We went to one extreme end of the airport and the tail of the plane was out over the grass. The engines roared deafeningly and the plane began to move slowly, feeling much like it was anchored to the ground.

We got up more and more speed, feeling each imperfection of the concrete as the plane complained about the unmerciful load on it. When we came to the warning lights that said we should be in the air we were still on the ground. I was looking out the window and saw the plane barely lift off just as we came to the grass—we narrowly cleared the trees and some buildings.

The pilot cleared his throat and said, "Uhmmm, well we are in the air. Our flight plan calls for us to fly at 35,000 feet this evening on our way to Harare, Zimbabwe. We should be in the air about eleven hours. We should arrive about six a.m. We will be flying over France, Spain and other nations in Africa. I will bring you up to date about our progress."

I kept feeling anxious and kept listening for the motors of the plane to throttle back as is common on most flights. After five hours in the air the motors were still running full throttle. I got up and asked the chief steward, "Say, is it common to load a plane like this one is loaded?"

He smiled weakly at me and said, "I have been a steward for years and I have never been on a plane that was loaded like we are. One comfort is that as we burn off the fuel we will get lighter and lighter." We talked on for a few minutes.

The pilot came on the intercom after we had been in the air for six or seven hours and said, "We finally made it up to 24,000 feet. It seems that is as high as she wants to fly tonight. It will get us there."

Exhaustion took over and we settled back for a few hours of rest as we covered most of the dark continent in the hours of the night. We were awakened very early the next morning for our breakfast that had been prepared for us in London.

When we landed at Harare the airplane shuddered and indicated its disapproval of the way it had been so overloaded.

Later I learned from one of my friends who is an engineer with Boeing, that the 707 is one of the strongest planes they ever built and is recognized for its ability to carry cargo.

Stepping off of the airplane in Harare, Zimbabwe, how different it is immediately hits the first-time visitor. It is as if one is visiting a different world than the one left in London.

Is it the air, the landscape, the people? I'm not sure. It just feels different. It isn't a feeling of danger, or a bad feeling, but one of dissimilarity. Maybe sort of like being projected in a time machine somewhere alien or ancient.

The countryside is different, the language is different, the smells are different, the people are different. Did I mention that the names are different? Not just different for animals, and these are different. The cow is no longer a cow, but a "mombe." Even a good old hippopotamus has a different name. I don't remember just what at the moment.

People's names are very different. It still came as a surprise when a big burly black man told me his name was "Precious." Was there ever a time when he was precious? Well, I suppose to his mother when he was very small. It did seem inappropriate for him now. I had no trouble remembering his name though. In fact, who could forget?

One man, who was a plumber, was named "Never." I'm told he was never there when you needed him. You could only count on the fact that he was never where he should have been. His name was rather prophetic.

I met another very black man who was talkative. I asked what his name was. You might have guessed, "Silence." Someone must have had a sense of humor. Anyhow it had worked out poorly in practice, for he was a talking machine.

Two children in one very large family were named, "Blessing" and "More Blessings." With so many children I wondered if they had run out of names, or were they truly thankful for so many?

Another common name in Zimbabwe is "Wireless." I guess it is true that people are wireless, but I usually think of someone that is wireless as having a loose wire. Or does it mean that they work without controls? Maybe the parents didn't know what it meant.

A lady told me one of her friends had a housemaid named "Mistake." I have seen some children whose parents thought they were a mistake, but this was the first time anyone I had known admitted it in naming the child. I wonder how this has left the child feeling about themselves.

One lady had tried hard to disguise her name and with good reason—it was Mrs. "Sithole." She pronounced it Si-toal-le. How was I to know that when I read it in print? The proper pronunciation somehow didn't strike me.

A bright-eyed young man said he was "Clever." I thought, I guess I had better watch myself with him, but really it was only his name. There were so many children in the family that they had run out of English sounding names and they probably did not know what it meant, only that it sounded good.

Twins were named "Mattress" and "Fatress." How would you like to be saddled with handles like that? What is a fatress? I wondered what the parents thought when they named their three children "Pilate," "Violet" and "Toilet." I am not pulling your leg, those were their names.

One of my favorite translators is named, "Sixpence." Everyone seems to think that is a right good name. Maybe you would consider naming one of your children "Half Dollar."

Bible names are common, such as "Shadrack," "Cephas" or "Meshack."

Imagine me trying to stifle my laughter when I was told a man's name was "Penis." Of course it was pronounced "Pee-on-us." Somehow that didn't really sound too much better. The doctor said that the prior sound had been given to it until so many people objected. Well, it was a good masculine name anyway.

Why did the parents decide to name their cute little girl "Office?" Was the mother working in an office? Was she born at the office, or did it sound businesslike? One pretty little girl was called "Lovemore." It is a good idea. The world sure could stand a lot more love, and it is a good reminder. How would you like to have a name that is a sermon?

Another man is named "Nobody." One fellow was introduced and I was sure I had misunderstood and had to ask again, "Pardon, what did you say?" He replied, "My name is Nervous Marbles." One was called "Silvernose." Another boy was called "Big Brain," while a rather scrawny man "Power Man."

Other names have beauty and meaning. "Simbarashe," power of God, or "Tinashe," the will of God. "Tarisha," look at what God has given us.

We could go on for "Evermore" about this subject. Yes, that was the name of another man. We might laugh at funny names, but each of these people really is "Precious" in God's sight. Every one of them is a "Blessing" and I suppose more of them would be "More Blessings." We all could "Lovemore" and more "Silence" would be "Precious." I don't know how the lady named "Plasida" fits into this whole story.

Every one of these people is known unto God. It gives me joy to know that each one of us will receive a new name in glory. Wouldn't it be too bad to be saddled with these names for eternity?

If I had not chosen to be a minister of Christ, would I have been able to travel like I have and meet these interesting people? Likely not. I thank God for having the chance to go to such interesting places and meet such "Precious" and "Clever" people. I hope the name "Lovemore" describes you.

On Location

Several years ago an historic meeting took place. African church leaders from an area covering nearly half of Zimbabwe gathered for the first time. Their purpose was to encourage each other by fellowship and Bible study. Many of them had very little if any formal theological education. Some of them did not even know how to read and write, but brought a scribe to do so for them. Often these older men are of great influence.

The meeting took place at the black church in Chinhoyi. The church building is in an area of town called the "Location." The church building is on the outskirts of town. After leaving the highway the road leads back over the hill past a school, along a dirt road around the side of the hill, and finally into the yard of the church.

The building is small—about fifty by seventy feet. It is made of cement block with a metal roof. The floors are polished concrete. Its meager furniture consists of simple pews made of bent pipe and boards with a few benches even more crude. There is a plain table for the Lord's supper and a fine pulpit in the form of a cross. The building has a very adequate and frequently used baptistery.

This area-wide meeting of the African evangelists, preachers, and elders is sponsored by the outstanding missionary, Dale

Marshall. Dale has worked with the people of Zimbabwe for a quarter of a century. One cannot travel far in any direction without seeing signs of his and his wife's Christian influence and ministry. By the standards of any first-world country, every church leader is below the poverty level.

The evangelists, considered the most prosperous of the group, ride 185 Honda trail bikes. These are provided by the Marshalls and the Central African Mission. The rest of the group have come from as far away as 186 miles. Most have ridden the bus or walked.

There is not one automobile owned by any of the lot of them. It appears that much of their clothing was owned by someone else before them. It is usually ill fitting, worn out and patched or mismatched. The exception is the evangelists who are paid by the Mission. They receive a meager, but fair salary and are able to maintain a somewhat higher level of existence.

Watching the men's feet as they come in is a study in the bottom edge of poverty. Some are barefoot, others have the most dilapidated, misfiting shoes imaginable, while there are a few who have good, proper sized shoes. Many go barefoot until near the church where they then put on their shoes.

When I asked Cephas, my translator, to read a passage from the Bible in Shona to the people, he said, "Oh, I haven't been able to see to read for over three years." Later I pursued the conversation, "Cephas, are you telling me you are going blind?" He replied, "Yes, three years ago I did a lot of translating and I haven't been able to read since."

I asked, "How old are you?" He said, "Forty-eight." It is really hard to judge their ages. "You mean you haven't been able to see well since you were forty-five?"

"That's right."

I took off my trifocal glasses and handed them to him, asking him to put them on. I explained how they worked and gave him my Bible. With an exclamation he said, "It is a miracle, I can read even the finest print!"

I told Cephas about a conversation I had with my eye doctor when I was forty-five. I felt for sure I was going blind. It is a normal part of the aging process. We sent Cephas off to the eye doctor and in two weeks he was fitted with glasses.

The black preachers are willing students, ready to learn, full of questions, excited about studying the scriptures and related subjects. We covered basic principles of discipleship and the basics of Textual Criticism, showing why the Bible is the Word of God. During the twenty hours of instruction they learned why the Bible is the inspired Word of God, from beginning to end.

One of the preachers gave an exclamation, peculiar to the Shona people, "Oh, why didn't someone tell us these things before?" Those who could write took copious notes, especially of where scriptures could be found about subjects of special interest to them.

The classes were offered all day long. They were offered the chance to vote if they wanted to have the sessions from 3 to 5 in the afternoon. At that time of day it was very hot and uncomfortable in the building. They voted to have the classes. Of the approximately one hundred people, only two or three wanted to dismiss the classes for a break. It would not be possible to find a more motivated class of learners than these men. Many sat on a narrow seat, a board nailed on round sections cut off a small tree.

Most of them are really godly. They have large gaps in their knowledge and Christian practice. The African Preacher's Conference helps them to make giant strides to correct this problem.

Feeding the Physical Body

The diet of these African church leaders at home consists of most modest fare. Their meals contain mainly sudza, a white corn meal mush so thick that it can be eaten with the fingers. If the family is eating extravagantly they will have a few scraps of meat, beef, mutton, or chicken. The quality of the meat is such that most of us would call it waste, or not fit for consumption, or we would make ground meat out of it. None of those from the bush, the rural area, are fat.

We sat down to a meal with them at the conference. The missionary and I ate about 20% of our bowl of sudza, dipping it into the greasy broth provided. The preacher sitting next to us asked if we were going to finish it off. We said, "No." He cleaned up the rest. They ate like they had never seen food before. The amounts of food consumed is almost beyond belief. We felt for sure they were taking some away for later use.

The seventy-three men and about twenty-five women and children consumed the following amounts of food from Tuesday evening through Sunday noon: 500-plus pounds of mealy meal, when cooked with the necessary water would make over a ton of sudza; 470 pounds of beef; copious amounts of vegetables; 58 large cabbages; 70 large bundles of rape (a kind of cabbage); large vats of tea; 48 loaves of bread; 20 large tins of jelly; 20 pounds of butter; 60 pounds of sugar; and several other things.

The bread was eaten with large amounts of butter and jelly. The two slices were about the size of a quarter of a loaf of bread. This was their mid-morning and mid-afternoon snack.

After a bit of calculation, my conclusion was that one lesson we had taught them was one in practical gluttony. The amount of food they ate was almost beyond my ability to conceive.

Results

Following the first preacher's conference the preachers baptized 97 people in the following thirty days. One preacher, Michael, said that due to the excitement he felt he had been able to begin two new churches in the following six months. The results from the labors of these preachers is spreading the gospel across the rural areas of the nation.

At the closing session on Sunday morning the building was filled. The seats were packed and crowded. The benches were full. People were sitting on the floor shoulder to shoulder.

At the conclusion of my final message on Sunday morning

20 people were baptized. These came in the major part from the work of the African preachers among their own people.

Chidamoya Compound

We had slept somewhat fitfully in anticipation of our early breakfast call and departure to the mission compound at Chidamoya. It was a bright Zimbabwe morning and there was a cool breeze that would soon be gone and replaced with near oppressive heat. It continued to grow hotter as we traveled to our assignment. We were traveling to a much lower elevation.

The Marshalls are the ultimate host and hostess and had everything prepared for the hot and dusty journey we had before us.

We loaded everything into their Mercedes Benz, not nearly new, but in a good state of repair for its year. We would take it instead of the mission pickup because it would smooth out some of the bumps on the last 59 miles of dirt road we were to maneuver.

The road north from Chinhoyi had an amazing amount of traffic on it for the early hour of the day. Huge lorries, belching black smoke, lumber along, driving (as far as we Americans are concerned), on the wrong side of the road. The exhausts of the large trucks and busses were aimed to the center of the road and blew about the height of the windshield of the car, or into your open window when they pass.

There were rolling hills and very soon we began to see the little round huts with cone-shaped grass roofs. Most of the African people live in these little houses called rondovals.

The paved road began to narrow and became only wide enough for one car. The oncoming traffic had to take to the shoulder, with the most daring driver taking the most of the blacktop.

The road soon gave way to just two black stripes of pavement about one foot wide, spaced right for cars wheels, too narrow for a truck or bus. Soon this gave way to gravel and very soon to dirt.

Dust billowed out from under the car and blocked our vision from behind and when some other vehicle passed us. Even though it is extremely hot and the car had no air conditioning, we had to roll up the windows to protect ourselves from the clouds of dust.

It was impossible to travel very fast due to the washboard condition of the roads. The rolling hills were dotted from time to time with small huts among the trees. Between the frequent rocky places were fields that would soon be planted to maize. A large number of African people were waiting along the road for the busses that run regularly. These busses are their only method of transportation, other than foot or oxcart.

No one seems to be in a hurry, except one young boy who we came upon who had been running his father's oxen. They were pulling a primitive wagon loaded with several other black boys. The oxen were foaming at the mouth and thoroughly lathered up. This was the only hurried activity we saw during the days we were in the bush. It appears boys everywhere are the same, they like to drive fast.

After what seemed like more than a hundred miles we descended a long hill and made our way up the other side of the mountain. At the top we came to Chidamoya Township. It is comprised of about ten buildings of ancient design. They are small, with no windows, dirty, with a few people standing around or leaning in the doorways.

The shacks are made of homemade brick overlaid with stucco. One has a sign on it, "Chidamoya Beer Hall." Nearby is another small building with the sound of a grinding mill rumbling from within. It was the sound of maize being ground to make flower for sudza, a staple of their diet.

In about two miles a large, beautifully-finished sign says, "Chidamoya Church of Christ Mission." It is a bit of civilization in the wilderness.

The mission had begun in 1936. This was due in part to the efforts of a black man of vision named Shadrack. He is now an old man and still dedicated to his Lord Jesus. When I had a chance to talk with him he said, "What do you think of this fine hospital?" He spoke pretty good English. I assured him, "It is really splendid. I was sure surprised to find it back here in the bush." He told me the story of how it had all begun.

As a young chief he had realized that if his people were ever to escape from the poverty, disease, and hardship that was their lot it would have to come through education. He saw that the only chance for education was the Christian missionaries. He made them welcome and urged them to come preach. He had heard the Christian story as a boy and had believed in Jesus as Lord.

I said to him, "People live a little differently here than they do where I come from." Shadrack replied proudly, "We live just like we have for over seven thousand years, except for our hospital, school, and church." I could see how proud he was of the mission compound, and with good reason.

He went on to explain that he was thought to be disloyal to his people because of his desire for the church and hospital, and had spent over a year in jail for his part in bringing the Christian Mission to Chidamoya.

The compound consists of over 100 acres. The hospital is built in somewhat of an odd shaped H, with open verandas and porches on several sides. Its construction is of brick with a corrugated metal roof. The floors are of polished cement. Otherwise it is quite primitive.

Originally it had been built at an expense of $100,000. During the war of independence it was burned down, leaving only the walls and floor. After the war it cost $200,000 to repair it and put it back in operation.

Electricity is supplied by an antiquated diesel powered generator. Water comes from two wells (called "bore holes") with small one-cylinder diesel motors that run part of the day to pump water into a large tank on the hill. The area is very dry except during the rainy season that lasts only a few weeks in summer.

The hospital is basically an outpatient clinic, except for two wings of beds, one for men and boys, the other for women and children. No meals are served by the hospital staff, but by the family members that come along to the hospital to help care for the patients. These people camp outdoors near the hospital and cook and help care for their family members who are in the hospital.

People who come for treatment come from as much as two to three hundred miles or more. They come in by foot, bus, or ox cart. Each patient is accompanied by as many family members as can come along. They care for the physical needs—food, laundry or other things that might be needed. It is like an extended vacation.

There was one doctor, Dr. Gloria Cobb, and several African nurses. Most of these nurses are finishing their nurse's training and have to serve in this remote area as a requirement for completion of their education. They learn good medical practice from Dr. Cobb.

Each day the hospital is surrounded by hundreds of people waiting for the recovery of their family member's health, or waiting for treatment themselves. Most of the people are camped around the compound in crude shelters or out of doors.

One patient, a young lady of twelve years, had dropped a water bucket on her foot. The bucket had fallen off her head and made a nasty cut on the top of her arch (very few of the people ever wear shoes).

We watched as the doctor supervised the cleaning and sewing up of the wound. I asked Dr. Cobb, "Can she return home now?" She said, "Oh no! Infection would set in and she would probably die from it. She must stay here until she is thoroughly healed. With all the dirt and germs and the way the people live she would never recover if I let her go home."

She would stay for the next 60–90 days camped near the hospital and receive treatment as it was needed. Her family would cook their food over an open fire, get their water from a faucet near the light plant, and wait.

The sight of the lines of sick people is enough to bring pity to the hardest heart. At the same time, it is a dramatic evidence of the power of the love of Christ as expressed through Christian people who make the hospital possible.

I asked Dr. Cobb, "What would have happened to the little girl otherwise?" She explained, "She would have been taken to the witch doctor who would have treated the foot with some medication like cow dung or a dirty black paste made up of grease and charcoal. She would have become infected and probably most certainly have died in a few days or a week or two.

She went on to explain that the most common disease she treated was infection, but she also treated TB, malaria and all sorts of venereal disease, often seeing patients with AIDS.

Dr. Cobb cheerfully goes about her almost insurmountable duties. Her radio telephone rings at all hours of the night and she will walk up the hill to the hospital or give directions to the nurse in charge. She is constantly training others to assist her in the more routine duties of medical care.

She regularly treats illnesses that are never seen by doctors in America, and this without the aid of the modern equipment and drugs that are used by doctors in first-world countries. The miracles she and God work provide new hope for these primitive people.

What keeps a beautiful lady of such refinement at her post of duty in such difficult settings? I asked her, was she ever lonely? She said, "We are always so busy we have little time to be lonely or to think of ourselves."

I had been asked to come preach and teach. The compound church was being beset by several serious problems. One old African man and his sons felt they owned the church. They threatened to kill anyone who would not do what they wanted. Some of the church members were resorting back to witchcraft and animism, a worship of praying to their ancestors.

My translator, Oliver Marowa, was a fine elder in the church and the chaplain at the hospital. He was a fine godly man and spoke English perfectly. The red brick church stood near the hospital. It had a long porch across the front with large white columns supporting the roof. Inside the building were benches and cement floors. There were few of the modern conveniences we expect except a large baptistery, much as could be found in many churches in America.

About one hour before time for the people to gather for a service a large gong was rung by an old gentleman. He was dressed in ragged clothes and the most dilapidated pair of shoes I had ever seen. The gong could be heard for miles around. The old gentleman had thick glasses that looked homemade. The lenses were like nothing I had ever seen and were fastened in by a white substance that made his eyes look like those of an owl. He had a big smile and his teeth showed his age, as decay had left them like stumps. He could speak no English, and all we did was shake hands and smile at each other.

People began to arrive early and continued to come and go for the duration of the services. My duty was to teach on the subject of discipleship. Teaching by an interpreter and cross cultural is difficult at best. The people were ready to learn and were intelligent. It was an entirely positive experience.

Many unexpected questions were asked during the question-and-answer period. One lady asked, "I am a widow; my husband died two years ago. A leader in a church nearby wants me to become his wife. I will be his second living wife. Should I marry him?" Polygamy is widespread.

I tried to explain that God had only made Adam one wife and Eve only one husband. Whenever polygamy came into a family it brought heartache. She should seek a husband that would love and care for her alone. It is a difficult problem, for men often die young and leave their wives destitute. Her chances of marriage were very poor and she had very few other alternatives than to marry as a second or third wife.

We helped in every way we could during our stay. I repaired the leaking faucets in the houses and helped put a ridge cap on a leaking roof. Each night we slept under a thin sheet with the windows open. We were confronted by the little lizards and spiders that looked the size of a silver dollar.

In the distance we could hear the sound of the ritual drums of the witch doctors. The drums were being sounded to keep away evil spirits from those who had died recently or for the first anniversary of someone's death.

This all reminded us that there was still a strong satanic influence and that Christ had only just begun to bring these primitive people out of their superstition and paganism.

God will most certainly add the names of Dr. Gloria Cobb and Margaret Dennis to His long list of faith heroes. They are helping to bring the people from the stone age into modern times. They are helping not only to save their physical lives but to bring them eternal salvation. When the gospel comes into the people's lives they are made beautiful. Hope shines in their faces. They begin to live better.

Where could a person better invest their lives than in such worthy ventures for Christ? Few other vocations would have offered us the opportunities to travel and be useful to mankind like the ministry.

Mono Pools

The mission field is not all work. After a very heavy schedule of teaching and preaching a few days of safari were planned. By the time we had started on our journey our excitement had grown almost beyond containment. We were headed for the Zambezi valley. If we had known all that we would encounter we would have been even more excited . . . and very nervous.

Our diesel safari vehicle was loaded to capacity with camping gear, clean water, food, tents, and sleeping bags. Behind was our little camp trailer filled with cooking utensils, gas lanterns and every imaginable kind of camping gear.

We were leaving civilization far behind and there would be no place to purchase anything. There would be no doctors, petrol or anything else that an emergency might require. What we needed we had to take along for the several days in the bush.

About 24 miles before leaving the paved road we began a steep descent down what is called the escarpment. We could see that we were entering a large valley—the Zambezi River valley. The temperature began to soar and we were thankful that we had dressed in our walking shorts and cool cotton shirts.

We had followed the paved road for about 92 miles before we turned onto a gravel road. In a few yards we came to a strong gate made out of a railroad track. There were armed guards at the gate and we had to produce our permit in order to enter the Mono Pools Game Preserve. Only fifty vehicles at a time are allowed to be in this gigantic park.

We traveled 65 miles before we came to a second gate. Again we were stopped by the guard to check our permits. After this gate we traveled another 53 miles along the washboard road and through billowing clouds of dust before we reached our campsite next to the Zambezi River.

There are many baobab trees along the roadside. They are giants of the plant world. Sometimes the base can be 20 or more feet through. Legend has it that the trees were so proud of their size and beauty that God pulled them up by the roots and planted them upside down. Their limbs are very much like what one can imagine roots should look like if stuck up in the air. One tree we stopped to observe, had a huge cavern inside, easily large enough for a family or two to live in.

We had seen no other vehicle or any sign of civilization for over 64 miles. Billows of dust wafted up from behind our diesel vehicle. We had long since quit trying to resist it and accepted that we were to be covered with dust and bugs as long as we were on safari. We had been taking quinine for several weeks in anticipation of this very journey. Otherwise we would have been in serious danger of malaria.

As we traveled deeper into the park and nearer the Zambezi River plain we were met by animals of many kinds and descriptions. There were the nimble impalas. There were many waterbuck all along the road. Monkeys of several varieties and sizes could be seen everywhere playing in the trees and running along the ground. Guinea hen are plentiful. The mighty elephants come lumbering along with their trunks swinging lazily back and forth.

We checked in with the park ranger. We asked several questions about the park and tried to make out his replies. He spoke very limited English, and I no Shona. He told us where we were to camp. We asked if any animals were permitted to be killed in the park. He said only when they were over populated. He said, "We have been having a real problem with poachers who are killing our rhinoceros."

I asked, "What do you do about the poachers?" He said quite matter-of-factly, "We shoot them." I asked, "Then what do you do with them?" He replied, "The animals clean them right up." We realized that we were now living by the rules of the jungle as we were no longer in civilization.

Someone had already settled into our camp site. It was a German tourist who had decided that the spot he had been assigned was not as good as ours. We asked him to move so we could camp and he swore at us.

We returned to the camp ranger. He came back with us to try to convince the squatter to move from our assigned place. We offered to take the other campsite, but the ranger said we could not do so as we were going to stay longer than the German, and another group would come to take the other place the next day, and we would have to move again.

Finally after two hours of haggling the man began to slowly take down his tent and move his camp. By then it was pitch dark—10 p.m.—and we had to set up our camp in the dark. Have you recently set up two large tents in the dark? We felt more than a little put out with the pushy and obnoxious man.

Our intruder had acquired some female African companionship for his camp-out—a young black prostitute. She was along to help work and provide additional sport for him. We learned later that many of these black temptresses were infected with AIDS or other venereal diseases. It seems that things have a way of, as people say in Zimbabwe, "sorting themselves out." I have since prayed for this unruly and selfish young man and wondered what his future had in store for him.

We fell into bed exhausted at 11 p.m. This was a mercy as we were surrounded by night sounds—frogs, and the giant elephants that kept swaying along past our tents. We heard hyena in the darkness nearby. We checked the sound of some large animal grazing near our tent, and found a giant hippopotamus grazing. They spend their days in the river underwater protecting their tender skin. Their nights were spent in grazing on the grass near the river.

In the morning the first sound we heard was the patter of something on the tent. It sounded like rain and some small stones falling from the sky. Upon investigation we found that the monkeys in the trees above were caring for their kidney and intestinal needs. The sign was all around the tent.

As we looked at the dusty ground outside our tent, there was not one square foot that did not have many animal tracks in it. Our tent had been passed by most of the animals of the forest. We had slept securely behind nothing more than our mosquito netting.

After we had cooked and eaten our breakfast we decided to take a hunting trip armed only with our cameras. Our safari vehicle had a platform on the roof for us to mount so that we could better view the wild animals. During the day we saw an array of animals—elephants, lions, hippopotamus, all sorts of rodents, deer, kudo, cape buffalo, snakes, anthills of gigantic proportions, and birds that we could not name.

The area is filled with wildlife much like what I could imagine the Garden of Eden must have been like when God first created the earth. The animals do not seem to be afraid of people or of the vehicles.

We took a midday siesta during the heat of the afternoon. As evening began to turn to dusk the largest bull elephant I had ever seen came lumbering right towards our tent.

I felt the chill of fear mount up in my throat. This effect did not strike my wife as she ran for the camera saying, "I want to get a close-up of him." Her little flash camera had at best a range of 15 feet. She ran towards this monster with me shouting for her to run the other direction. She ran right towards him flashing the bright light in his eyes. (African elephants are untameable and very dangerous. They will grab a person with their trunk and impale them on their tusk.)

I expected him at any moment to reach out with his swinging trunk and grab her and impale her, which is what would be a natural response to a woman flashing bright lights in his face. Instead he seemed rather bored by the whole process, and annoyed by this intrusion into his journey to the mighty Zambezi for his evening swim. (Margaret did get close enough to get a picture!)

The next day we wanted to try our luck fishing for tiger fish in the river. This presented several problems; one was negotiating the mud-flats near the river and the other watching out for crocodiles and trying to fish without getting our hands or feet in the water. The water is infected with bilharzia.

Bilharzia infects people with liver or brain flukes, or worms. It can make one very ill, and we had already decided that we would take every precaution to keep out of the water.

We made the mistake of taking one of the ladies along on this fishing trip and she caught by far the biggest fish. It must have been 24 inches long and probably weighed 10-12 pounds. She insisted that we take it back to be cooked. My stomach didn't agree that this was a good idea, but she insisted so we agreed.

That evening when we had finished cooking our beef steaks on the grill over the open fire we prepared the fish to be cooked. We got it started and it began to smell really good. It was a mild white meat and smelled like a delicacy as it cooked over the fire.

The ladies decided that it was time for their evening constitutional and they departed for the comfort station that was about a quarter of a mile from our campsite. It was now pitch dark with only our gas lantern giving off light near our tents. They took only one small pocket-size flashlight with them and started off chattering like a flock of magpies. We continued our conversation by the fire as we watched our tiger fish cook.

Suddenly we heard a blood-curdling scream come out of the darkness. It was followed by more screams from more than one of the ladies. We grabbed the large flashlight and ran towards the screaming. Guns and large knives are forbidden in the park. We met three of them running towards us. One, my wife, was missing and still was setting up a sound that would almost wake the dead.

Together we hastily proceeded to rescue her. We found her intact and unharmed, other than scared out of her wits. She had been in a hurry to get to the rest room and had led out in front of the flashlight. Seeing her own shadow, she had imagined that it was a hyena. Once frightened she could not think and the ladies who carried the flashlight had run, leaving her in the dark with her fears.

We were considerably relieved by her safety and continued on to the rest rooms, as their protectors. We returned straight away to the fire to find that in our absence the hyena had eaten our fish, all that was left was one small piece, just enough for us to try a taste of it. It was delicious. Did you ever share a meal with a hyena? This ministry thing can have its dull spells.

When we were out fishing we decided that rather than to walk back the three-quarters of a mile to the truck through the sand and mud we would walk back directly to the woods and then along the higher solid ground.

As we started towards the brush I asked, "What will we do if we meet some cape buffalo?" Cape buffalo are the second most dangerous creatures in Africa, second only to the crocodiles. I was told that we hadn't seen any cape buffalo and there probably weren't any in the area at the time. I was told, "Dale Marshall said, we should be safe, but I sure don't have any desire to meet any buffalo."

We walked along talking about the cunning of the buffalo.

They have been known to track human beings and even to hide in the brush, backtracking on their own trail to attack humans.

I had my eyes carefully peeled to watch for any movement in the brush. I could not believe my eyes—not more than fifty yards from us stood four huge cape buffalo with their heads lowered, watching our every move. I stopped in my tracks and was bumped into by those following me. Breathlessly I pointed to what I saw. Dale turned white and turned and ran as hard as his legs could carry him—he had to really run for I was right on his heels. We ducked over the bank of the river and set a new record for running in loose sand.

When we returned to our vehicle we still had not regained normal color nor heart rate.

During that night we were greeted by a constant menagerie of wild animals. We waited with our flashlights ready to shine at whatever came by.

As we returned to civilization we came to the paved road and came to a road block. The road block was to spray our vehicle for the tsetse fly, the carrier of sleeping sickness. It was another reminder of the remote area we were leaving.

Our time at Mono Pools was too short. We left with a new appreciation for the wonders of nature. My thoughts were, "And our Lord Jesus Christ created all of these things for us." How can anyone see such creations and not believe in God? "The things that are made declare His everlasting power and divinity, so that they are without excuse."

Meaning

Our times in Zimbabwe were meaningful; not because we saw strange sights, nor because we experienced strange culture, nor because we had a chance to see the many creations of God.

What gave real purpose to the travel? It was the chance to minister and work in ways that make a difference in people's eternity—the chance to teach church leaders from across the nation, to give them formal theological education, to teach them to be better soul winners, to teach them how to organize a church into an effective working unit for teaching and evangelism. The chance to teach the men why the Bible is the inspired word of God was gratifying. This effort was life transforming, eternity-changing labor. This gave rich satisfaction.

What a blessing to preach and teach and then witness the people lined up across the front of the building and down the sides responding to the invitation. What could be more meaningful than to see these people coming in faith to make the good confession and be buried with the Lord in Christian baptism.

Their lives had given them very little earthly pleasures, but they now were children of the King and prepared for a mansion in heaven. What satisfaction to hear the comment of the black evangelist who said, "I got so excited about the work of the Lord that I began two new churches." He had begun to tithe—something rather new for the very poor African Christian. His farm had begun to prosper and his farm was the highest producing farm in the area the past year. He gave the praise to God who had blessed him because he had stepped out in faith to tithe.

The black evangelists also reported 100 baptisms in one month following the training. This kind of result has continued for many months and continues to this day. This gave us a deep sense of satisfaction for our small investment.

These are not converts made by high powered American evangelists, but by people from the community winning their neighbors and friends. At the conclusion of this mission trip, a ten-day evangelistic meeting was held at the English speaking church.

This revival produced many baptisms, renewals of faith, commitments, and conviction of sin that were expressed in rededication and tears of repentance.

Several families from ranches ranging from 2,700 to 5,000 acres came with their husbands, wives and children, to give their lives to the Lord.

In retrospect, why did we received these rich blessings, why did a farm boy from back in the foothills of the Cascades

Mountains of Oregon have such valuable experiences? It could only be that the ministry is still one of the most exciting and worthwhile works that can be undertaken by a person wanting meaning in their lives. That must be why God, who had only one boy, made Him a preacher of righteousness.

    Is the ministry still a valid way to serve humanity and God? If it isn't, there isn't anything in life worthwhile. Want to travel? God will put you on wings if you give your life to His service.

Ministry and Travel

Ministry has taken us from coast to coast, to Canada, Mexico, to England, Germany, Austria, Holland, Italy, Jordan, Lebanon, Syria, Israel, Kenya, Zimbabwe, Greece, the Greek Islands, Turkey, Denmark, and memory fails me where else.

Each of these trips has provided opportunities for usefulness and the making of friends from many of the countries. Several of these friends stand out in our memories.

David

We met David first in Tel Aviv, Israel. He met us and helped us work our way through customs—no small feat at that time. The Ben Gurion airport's security system is one of the best in the world.

He immediately impressed us, having lots of energy in his rather rotund body. He was smiling, cheerful, ready to assist us in a genuinely helpful way. I thought to myself, this man is having a good day. He must have gotten a raise, or maybe he is about to be a grandad, or has inherited money.

The next morning we traveled north up the plains of Sharon towards Haifa. Each day of the seven days spent with him were filled with the cheerfulness of this bald, overweight, middle aged man.

I found he did not own a house or car. He was an Arab, not Jewish. His life was filled with perplexities from the viewpoint of we Americans. He lived in a financial system that was at that time experiencing 175% inflation.

Finally on the fifth day we spent with David I asked, "David, could you tell us where you get your energy and boundless optimism?"

He said, "I sure could and would be delighted to do so." We were walking in Jerusalem—there were about 17 of us. He said, "Step into this little cafe and let me buy you all a soda while I tell you."

This is David's story.

"When the Six-Day War broke out in Israel my wife and two children were visiting her sister in Damascus, Syria. It was most unfortunate timing as all travel and communication was stopped between the two nations. We could not write, phone, or communicate in any way."

"I had no idea of their fate, nor did they of mine. Every effort that I tried ended in failure. After six years of living alone and not knowing if they were dead or alive, I had come to the end of my rope."

"I had faithfully gone to the Mosque every day, sometimes as often as five times, and earnestly prayed for their return. It was as if I were praying to a rock. Nothing happened. I got more and more depressed. I was not doing well with my work guiding people around Israel."

"One day my heart was breaking. I was guiding a group of Christians from the United States. One of the group got me aside in the middle of the morning and asked me what it was that had left me so very depressed. I told him the story of my sad life."

"He prayed with me and suggested that I should go home that evening and address my prayers to the Father in the name of His Son, Jesus Christ."

"In two days I received a telegram from the Red Cross, and in seven days my wife and two children were home in Jerusalem."

David went on to explain, "I asked another

Christian to teach me, and upon my faith in Christ I was baptized, and now my wife and children are also Christians. This is the reason for the joy in our hearts. Mohammed is deaf, prayers addressed to the father in Jesus' name bring results."

Two years later I was sitting in a restaurant in Arad, Israel. I was eating a type of bird that I have still not identified. Could it have been stork or crane? All of a sudden I heard this cheerful voice, "Well hello Brother Crane. How has the Lord been treating you?"

I replied that God had been treating us very well. It was none other than David. I asked about his wife and family. He replied, "My son has just graduated from the University, and my daughter is going to be married next week. The Lord just keeps pouring out more and more blessings on our family."

I have not seen or heard from David since.

Ned *(Not his true name for reasons to be seen in this story.)*

We came ashore in Kushadashy, Turkey. We had a delightful trip on the 125-foot ferry from the island of Chios. We had enjoyed the azure blue waters of the Aegean Sea and the two to three hour boat ride.

The customs station was rather quaint, but did manage to check to see if we had the proper visas and passports. When they were all stamped we had lunch in a small cafe right on the harbor.

We were seated outdoors and had a constant battle to protect our food from the scavengering cats, dogs and seagulls. Nothing went to waste and they looked so hungry that we gave plenty of our food to them. We had been fed all too well and they looked nearly starved.

After eating we set out towards Ephesus, which was our main sight-seeing venture for the remainder of the day. We drove the 35 or so miles and arrived at one of the most spectacular ruins in all of Turkey.

The city was built at four different locations over the years.

We were mainly interested in the city that was visited by the Apostle Paul, and later became the home of the Apostle John.

The city at the time of Paul and John had an estimated population of 250,000 and was nestled along the Aegean sea in a beautiful harbor. The city declined and was deserted because the harbor was silted in and the people driven from the area by the swamps and mosquitoes that occupied what had once been the harbor.

The reminders of the glorious past of this city are everywhere. The small theater that would seat about 2,500, the large amphitheater that would seat about 25,000, the Agora or ancient marketplace, the library of the unbeliever Celces, all speak of the glorious past.

The temple of Diana and the marble streets and buildings all are reminders of the past grandeur. Today little remains but ruins that until recently were forgotten.

We were interested in this spot because of the influence that Christ had there. Paul's longest ministry was here and he said the gospel went out to all of Asia from this dynamic church.

The remains of the Church of Mary that had its roots in the church begun by Paul cover several acres and tell of the power and glory of the work of Christ there. The first worldwide council of the Christian church was held here.

This, though, is not the main story at this time. What sticks most clearly in my mind is our guide, Ned. Ned was a very well dressed debonair man of about 50 years. He has greying, wavy, dark hair. He was a typical example of a handsome Turk.

He knew the nation's history well; wanted to show us a good time, but lived on the edge of the law and what is right. It was not long before we discovered that he wanted to tell us what we wanted to hear. He wanted to deal in black market money to turn our American dollars into profit for himself. He was ready to take us to his friends to buy merchandise from which he received a sizeable kickback.

Even though we knew he wouldn't hurt us and he fit into the

image of a suave and wise man of the world looking out for number one, we knew he couldn't really be trusted as we had trusted David.

What was the difference? I took Ned aside out on the balcony of our beautiful hotel, the Oteli Ephes Diana in Izmir. When we were seated looking out over the beautiful semicircle harbor I asked, "Ned, what do you know about Jesus Christ? You seem very familiar with the New Testament. Has anyone taught you about Jesus?"

He replied, "Charles, I have thoroughly studied the teachings of the New Testament. I am thoroughly convinced that it is the truth and that Christianity is the only true religion. But if I were to be a Christian here in Turkey I would be persecuted and could not enjoy the standard of living that I do. One of these days when I get financially more secure, I am going to give my life to Jesus Christ."

I asked, "Ned, what if you die before that? Ned, what about the influence you are having on your wife and children? What will God say to you at the Judgment when you knew what was right and didn't do it? What about the stand of Paul that caused him to be whipped and jailed in the very city that you guide people through each week?"

He said, "I know, I know, I'm just not ready to make a commitment."

We then understood why Ned was unhappy, basically egocentric and worried about the future. He had made bad choices about the Lord.

When we returned some six years later I could find no one that knew of him. My prayer is that this conversation on the balcony of the Oteli Ephes Diana made a difference in his life. Certainly a radical change was needed.

Egypt

In the third grade I found a library book with pictures of the Pyramids at Giza in Egypt in it. I was thoroughly fascinated by the pictures and the story about them. After that, the hope of seeing them in person never totally left my mind.

As already told, a minister's account of his Middle East travels deepened my interest in seeing the lands of the Bible. While still quite young the opportunity came to visit Egypt, followed by more than a dozen more trips there since.

On this particular trip I was accompanied by a physician friend, his wife, daughter, and one of her friends. We had spent the day in Luxor seeing the temple at Karnak and the Valley of the Kings. When we returned to the airport at noon for our return flight to Cairo we were told that our flight had been cancelled. When I told my doctor friend he said, "Oh, no, I am to be in surgery back home in three days and my schedule is full for days."

I said, "Well, there are other ways back to Cairo; let me see if I can find a way for us. I tried and learned that the train and boats were booked full for 40 days, the hotels were booked full, and a rental car was out of the question since the roads were closed due to a sand storm that had made them impassable. We were stuck.

I returned to my friends and said, "Well, God must have us here for a reason; why don't I see if I can find out why." Our flight had been cancelled because the President of Egypt had commandeered the airplane for some government use. We were stranded in the small Luxor airport with about 300 other passengers. No other flight was anticipated that would accommodate us for several days.

I began to look through the crowd for someone who spoke English. I tried several until one man said he did. He was dressed in a blue pinstriped three-piece suit and we began to visit. We learned we were the same age, that each had three children, the oldest of which was a daughter with two younger boys. We introduced ourselves and I learned that his name was Safwat Sadek, an attorney and also a general in the Egyptian army.

I asked him if he were a Christian and he said no, he was Muslim. I asked if he would mind if I talked to him about why I believed Jesus was the Messiah and Savior. He agreed, and I took out my small pocket Bible from my vest pocket and took him through the prophecies of the Old Testament and gave him a summary of the Gospel from the New Testament. We began about 3 PM and talked for about six or seven hours, seated in the corner of the airport. At 11:30 PM it was announced that a jumbo jet that had missed its other connection had landed, and there was room for about 200 of the 300 people.

My doctor friend, wife, girls, and I linked arms and did the flying wedge and found seats on the plane. When we were seated, lo and behold, if Safwat was not seated next to me. We talked all the way back to Cairo. When I returned home, a letter awaited me asking that now that he was a believer, what did he need to do to do to become a Christian? I told him what was needed and he was baptized, and we remained friends for many years until his death.

I was invited back to be present for his oldest son, Sama's, betrothal ceremony. I was treated like royalty, being housed in a fine hotel and enjoying dinner in their home. The betrothal ceremony was more elaborate than any wedding I had ever attended. After the ceremony, a banquet lasted until 3 AM the next day.

His daughter, Azza, worked for the department of antiquities of Egypt and agreed to take me to visit important archaeological sites, one of which was the Coptic museum in Cairo. I wanted to see the Nag Hamadi ancient texts that are in the Coptic museum. When we arrived I was introduced to the curator of the museum and he permitted me to look at and photograph these old rare manuscripts.

He asked if I would like to meet the head of the Coptic Seminary and church historian, Zaki Shenuda. (Zaki had written the seven-volume history of the Coptic Church, telling me that Mark, the writer of the second Gospel, had begun the church in Egypt.) I was delighted to do so and the two of us discussed church history and current events for about an hour. He then asked if I would like to meet the head Bishop of the Coptic churches worldwide. I jumped at the chance.

I was ushered into a large office with walls lined with shelves of books and was introduced to a very impressive man in a long robe, with long flowing beard whose name was Constantine Gregorious. He apologized, saying he was very busy and could only spare about 15 minutes.

We began to discuss church doctrine and world events, and three hours later I was begging to be excused, since Azza was sitting waiting for me. I was able to explain to him my concept of restoring biblical Christianity by returning to New Testament teachings and practices. He heartily agreed this was what must happen. We talked of Christian baptism and the observance of the Lord's Supper. Their practice is believer's baptism by immersion and the weekly observance of the Lord's Supper.

Later that day, when I was reunited with my friend Safwat, he expressed his surprise that we had gotten to see such an important church leader, saying he had never seen him except on television.

When a person sets out to serve the Lord with a pure heart, there are wonderful and important events that will impact their lives and influence the work of the church worldwide. Such events happening to a preacher from a small church in Douglas County, Oregon, illustrate how important ministry for Christ is how He can use even an unimportant young preacher if he is willing serve Him.

An Interest that Began at Age Thirteen

Homer

As a boy of thirteen I was building fence on the back of our farm that was situated back in the beautiful foothills of the Cascade Mountains of Oregon. These mountains are noted for their Douglas Fir trees, crystal-clear mountains, streams and lakes. It was a nearly ideal place for a boy to be raised.

We usually carried a gun as we never knew if we would be confronted by a bear, mountain lion, or grey digger squirrel. On this particular spring day my companion was my Scotch collie dog Captain, a post-hole digger, rolls of barbed wire, other assorted tools and our Ford tractor.

I was busily at work when I heard the sound of a Caterpillar tractor coming in the distance. Soon I saw what appeared to be a brand new track-laying tractor pulling a huge Douglas fir tree behind it down one of our farm roads that came out of the heavy forest.

My immediate thought was, someone is stealing our timber. I stood in the middle of the road until the tractor had to stop. Off of the tractor climbed one of the most handsome men I had ever seen. Most loggers, of which I had seen plenty, looked like they were born dirty and with ragged Levis cut off abut six inches too short, big red suspenders, hobnail boots and some sort of filthy hat and shirt that had been soaked with sweat and dirt.

But this was not the case. This man was dressed in dickey, tan colored pants and shirt, that were clean and pressed. The tractor looked like it was brand new, but in reality was years old and well used. Later I learned that this man even combed his hair before he went to bed.

I asked, "Whose log is that you are yarding down our road?"

He replied, "Your father has given me permission to yard some logs across your place so I do not have to build a road through the timber to where I am logging."

I said,

"My name is Chuck Crane."

He told me his name, Homer Moxley.

That began what has been one of my dearest friendship and continues on to this day. He was a man of about thirty-five years. I soon learned that he was of the Latter-Day Saint, or Mormon religion. Being a Christian myself this led to many discussions about the merits of the Christian and Mormon religions. He gave me my first Book of Mormon that I own to this day.

As a boy of thirteen I began to read the Book of Mormon, in the prescribed way, "Pray and ask with a sincere heart and God will show you if this is true." I did so and began to find many unbelievable things in this purported scripture.

Our conversations along with a number of other influences led Homer to make a firm commitment to the real Jesus and obey Him as Lord of his life. This was the beginning of what has been a life-long interest, the study of the Latter-Day Saints' religion.

Sally

About two or three years later the hormones began to kick in and I discovered girls. This was not to say that I had not previously noticed the gentler sex, but only that my back woods and Christian upbringing had made me more than cautious.

Finally the course of nature had its sway and I began to notice a very pretty and vivacious little gal named Sally. Her bright smile, boundless energy and bright blue eyes captivated my heart in what was to bloom into my first real romance. (This is really beside the real story, but is a necessary part of the story.)

We began to date and for me my whole social life was

wrapped up in school and church. I asked her to attend with me and was surprised to learn that her family were Latter-Day Saints. Since I have noticed how many LDS women are especially attractive and have decided it is their strong emphasis on physical and material things that caused them to give more attention to their appearance.

More than this was the case with Sally. She was graced with raw beauty and a vivacity that caused everyone to like her. We continued to date for most of the rest of High School.

Well, Mormons are not ashamed to witness to others. This led to long discussions with her family and before long she, her sister, Father and brother gave their lives to the real Jesus in obedience.

To this day I hold Sally in high regard for her fine qualities and high moral character. She developed into a fine Christian wife and mother. Her Christian faith has directed her life.

Lowell

At age sixteen the urge to get a steady, paying job consumed my mind. This led to my spending several days visiting every place in our small town that employed people and asking for a job. After visiting every place once and nearly making the rounds a full second time I was hired by a fine, upstanding man, Lowell Funk.

Lowell owned a tire shop that catered primarily to log trucks and vehicles that serviced the timber industry. Not only has Lowel remained a good friend to this day, we developed a mutual respect. He is a man of high character.

Yes, Lowell was Mormon. He was not only devout, but had attained a position of leadership in his church, I believe as high as Stake President, which means he had duties that related to more than one Ward or Church.

Again, our relationship led to discussions and later for Lowell to attend lectures that I gave on this subject. To this day Lowell remains committed to his religion, but our relationship is one of mutual friendship and respect. Here again, God was preparing for things to come.

Larry

Lowel withheld part of my paycheck while I worked for him and put it in the bank. Frankly, I was a little peeved but he was the boss, I needed the job and I had no alternative except to quit. His wisdom really paid off when I got to college. I had money for tuition and the practice of saving has stuck with me the rest of my life.

At college I met Larry Jonas, who was already much better read on the subject of the Mormon religion. We became friends and were soon visiting with Mormon people. Our efforts were earnest, but too bombastic to be as effective as they might have been. The best result was learning.

Dean

About the same time, I came in contact with a man at work whose name was Dean. (To protect his privacy his last name will remain unstated.) He again became a further part of my education. He held the High Priesthood of the LDS religion and had been on a mission. Since I worked around him I soon learned that he had a totally different set of values from those I had learned as a Christian.

His excuse always was, I am just like our Prophets Joseph Smith and Brigham Young. It was not right but was true, he was just like his Prophets. At this point in my life the pattern was clear, Mormon people all had one thing in common, the real spirit of Christian character and holiness was missing.

This is not to suggest that they were not good people by the standard of the world, but true-hearted godliness and a personal relationship with Jesus was missing from them all.

With this background I would like to give several brief biographies of people with whom I have shared a part in their coming out of the Mormon religion to know the real Jesus as Lord of their lives. The names have been changed to protect their privacy and because people who leave the LDS church often suffer severe family, social and financial persecution.

Lamar the Banker

Most LDS people are ready to give the testimony of their faith. Yes, it is a canned message and most all sound the same, but they tell the story of their church.

In addition, few religions do a better job of preparing their people to do a suave job of presenting their religion. They are cultured, well dressed, socially acute and diplomatic.

Lamar really impressed me from the very first meeting. He was the vice president of our bank. He was tall, handsome, lots of black hair, slicked back, a large warm smile with white even teeth, and a greeting and handshake that made me feel like a long-lost friend. Nothing appeared phony, this man was genuine I knew from the first visit. He believed what he believed.

In a few weeks I received a phone call at my church office asking if I would have lunch with him. This seemed logical since both my personal account and the church's bank accounts were in his bank.

He arrived in his Buick automobile, it was cleaned and polished. He was dressed in a dark pin-striped suit, with a well chosen tie, hanky in the coat pocket and looking ready for the photographer.

We drove to the country club. With a big smile he said, "Well, I hear preachers eat a lot of chicken, this is your chance to have a tenderloin steak or lobster. I believe I settled for a ribeye steak.

After a few minutes of idle talk he broached the subject;

"What do you think about the Book of Mormon and its claims as a second revelation of Christ for America?"

As a young preacher, not long out of Bible College, certainly not dry behind the ears, I was suffering from a certain amount of social and financial intimidation. My car, clothes and manners were deficient and I knew it.

My reply was, "Lamar, why don't you tell me about it. I would like to learn more." This was like saying sic-'em to my Scotch collie, Captain. He told me about the Book of Mormon,

Adventures of a Young Preacher

his conversion, his family's long history in the church, his mission, that he had served as Ward Bishop and Stake President. This only further intimidated me.

I could relate to David as he faced Goliath. I was not up to doing anything in my own strength or wisdom. My trust had to be totally in the Lord. I prayed silently for kind and wise questions that might start Lamar thinking.

As it came time for us to return to our jobs I asked,

"Lamar, I've been told that there have been nearly 4,000 changes in the Book of Mormon. That certainly can't be true, can it, since it was, as you said, 'translated by the gift and power of God.'"

His reply rather shocked me.

"No, it certainly can't be true. The Book of Mormon was and is the most correct book on earth."

Meekly I asked,

"Could we have lunch again and you research this for me, the evidence I have found seems pretty strong that the book has been changed a lot?"

With a big smile, Lamar replied, "I'll give you a call when I have the proof for you of the Book of Mormon's accuracy."

Because he was a truly honest man and of high intelligence, it was not long until we met again for dinner. This time we ate at a more modest place and I footed the bill. His first words after we had said grace over the meal were, "Charles, I'm pretty shocked at what I have found for you. The Book of Mormon has been changed, but nothing really important was changed, they were mostly just scribal errors."

I replied, "Oh, God didn't protect the writing process? I suppose he still doesn't protect the recording of the Prophet's revelations."

Lamar replied, "Oh, I see what you mean, we do have a minor problem here. I'll see what I can find out about this."

"Lamar, while you are at it, could you check another thing for me that I have been told?"

Adventures of a Young Preacher

"Sure, what is it?"

"Well I'm bothered by all the doctrinal changes in the revelation called the Doctrine and Covenants. I have found over 20 doctrinal changes and the first section or chapter says these revelations would never change."

"Sure, I'll check it out for you and we can meet again."

I heard nothing from Lamar for months. I saw him at the Bank, he was warm and friendly, but I thought, that is the end of that.

About two years later, while out of town for a speaking engagement, when I returned to the motel where I was staying, the light was blinking on the phone, indicating that I had a message. I called the operator and got this message.

"A Lamar called and said it is super important that you call him this very night, no matter how late it is when you get back to your room."

It was eleven p.m. when I called. Can you imagine my consternation at what Lamar had to say.

"Charles, some months back you got me thinking, and I have been unable to put all of this thing about changed scripture out of my mind. This has caused me to quietly go about checking out the evidence for the church that I had always accepted as gospel truth. I have grown more and more deeply grieved by what I have found. When will you be home?"

I told him I would be home some time Friday evening and he elicited a promise that I would come to their home directly after work, which I did. We studied the matter with the Bible, Book of Mormon and the other LDS scriptures until 3 a.m. when we went to the church where Lamar and his wife Cindy were immersed into Christ.

In the wee hours of the morning we prayed and rejoiced together that they had found a true relationship with Jesus, Lord of the universe. My final words to Lamar and Cindy were, "Please do not make waves about your new-found faith. Give yourself some time to settle into it before you take on the establishment."

I was overjoyed to find them Sunday in church and to rejoice in their being faithful Christians.

But the joy of their new life was too much for them. When they were questioned by church authorities as to why they had quit tithing they cheerfully responded, "we have left a cult and become true Christians."

About three months later I received a call from Lamar, he was very upset and said, "Can I see you in your office immediately?"

I replied, "Sure, come right down."

When he came in he looked haggard and like he had not slept at all the night before. In truth he hadn't. He told this story.

"Last evening before I left work the superiors of my Bank came to my office and presented evidence to me indicating that I had been embezzling money from my bank. They are insisting that I take a lie detector test tomorrow and if I don't I will be fired."

I said, "Lamar, have you stolen anything from the bank? I know the answer, but I want to hear it from your own lips."

"Charles, of course I have not stolen from the bank."

"Lamar, they must have found shortages or they would not have anything to accuse you about."

"Well, yes, they did find shortages, but no more than is normal in any bank. The tellers make mistakes in handing out money, sometimes petty cash is not reported accurately. In fact in the whole of last year there was less than $300 missing."

I asked, "What have past years been like and who has accused you?"

"This has been our best year in shortages, but they are accusing me for all money missing since I began to work for the bank ten years ago. I have been scrupulously honest and year after year gotten the award for being the best bank vice president."

I said, "Lamar, just take the lie detector test it will prove your innocence."

He answered, "I'm afraid to do so, this is a vendetta against me because of my leaving the Mormon church. The test will not be honest and no matter how I score they will prove me guilty."

Unfortunately, Lamar was right. At my and his wife's insistence he took the test, failed and was fired from his job. His whole world was coming apart around him. How was he to pay for his car, house, country-club membership and his lavish lifestyle?

The bank must have known they had a weak case against him, because he was never jailed and formal charges were not pressed against him.

Try as he might he could not find a job anywhere in the whole state. He had to move to another state and take a job as a checker in a super market. This was at greatly reduced wages and with terrible stress in his life.

I visited him about one year later and this handsome man with the big head of black hair was totally grey and was recovering from a heart attack.

The rest of the story is that after five years and spending thousands of dollars in attorney fees his name was cleared.

Someone had placed an employee to spy on Lamar on the staff of his bank and to find a cause against him. After months the only thing they could find was a trumped-up charge.

The employee who testified against him went to jail for perjury when the case eventually came to trial. Lamar had lost his life but found it.

The humble efforts of a young preacher, not too gifted, but genuine in his faith had helped deliver a family from the clutches of an evil system that proved its true nature when they chose to leave.

A great deal of satisfaction remains now after many years, realizing that even though many temporary things were lost to Lamar and his wife, the eternal things can never be lost.

"We just think we should visit a Christian Church before we are baptized in the Mormon Church."

A well-dressed and attractive couple came into church one Lord's day morning with their three children. They seemed to enjoy the service and visited in a friendly manner after the service.

As was my custom, I got their names and addresses from the roll call cards and called on them the very next evening. They told me that they had been studying with the missionaries and had decided to be baptized soon. I pleaded with them to wait until we could study with them.

Later in the week I returned at an appointed time and talked with them for several hours until they began to express serious doubts about their decision to become Mormons.

Ed said to me, "Well, you have made the LDS look pretty bad here, but I am wondering how it would look if you had to face some of their big guns. I bet things would be quite different."

His wife Jean chimed in, "Charles, if you are so sure of what you are saying, would you be willing to meet with their main Ward teachers?"

My thought was, I have really gotten myself into a mess this time. But I had no choice, either put up or shut up. I agreed and then went home to a sleepless night.

In the morning I called a trusted friend, Marv Cowan. He was a bit older and had extensive experience with the Mormons. I asked, "Marv, would you be willing to go with me to the slaughter?"

His response cheered my failing heart, "You bet I would go, I'd love to!"

The appointment was made for the following Tuesday evening. The Ward teachers were a bit apprehensive, but got the same prodding from Ed and Jean that I had received.

The evening came. I had applied several extra layers of antiperspirant. In short, the meeting was a total blow out of the Mormon leaders. They looked so foolish that they began to brag about how fast their church was growing and how many members they had.

Marv's reply shocked me, "I am still a member and belong to such and such a Ward."

The meeting came to an end and my deodorant had held and I slept much better than I had for several days.

About six weeks later I received a call from Marv.

"Charles, would you go as a character reference to my excommunication trial? I do not know what this is all about, but I am being charged and tried."

"Of course I'll go, when is it?"

"Well, they must be anxious because it is this very coming Sunday at 3 p.m."

The Sunday came and we were unsure of what to expect. Marv first was charged with false doctrine and joining another church. He asked what kind of proof they had that he had joined another church. This led to the Mormon leaders looking at each other and then asking, "Aren't you a Christian preacher?"

Marv's reply was, "I refuse to testify against myself. What is your proof?"

Everything came to a standstill. Embarrassment was shown on the Bishop's face, the same man we had so resoundingly shown wrong a few weeks before at Ed and Jean's home.

Ed and Jean as well as about fifty other Christians were in the audience.

Finally, Marv said, "Do you have a telephone directory?"

They produced one and he said,

"Look up my name in the church section and you will find your proof, I am listed as a preacher there. I have refused to answer to demonstrate that you often proceed without evidence or proof, this is just another illustration of the lack of credibility and evidence you have."

Since I had come as a witness I was asked by the judge if I had anything to say. I replied that I did and said, since they normally are hesitant to excommunicate someone except for serious moral infractions, "Does your unchurching Marvin mean that you are saying he is not a fine Christian man?"

The judge replied, "Oh of course not."

I replied, "Then I have only one more question, is it the practice of the Mormon Church to remove fine Christian men from your church?"

To this question the whole audience responded with laughter. And Marvin was excommunicated.

One can go into the lion's den of false religion armed with truth and need not fear. After this time my efforts took on a new boldness, tempered with kindness and love, well most of the time.

The Missionaries at the Door

It was one of those rainy Douglas County mornings when the mountains to the east and west were shrouded in clouds. The drizzle had continued now for days and the whole area around our small town had begun to look like a swamp. Water was standing everywhere.

Imagine our surprise when two young men dressed in black slacks, white shirts, ties and rain slickers showed up at our door. We lived at the end of a long lane and the lane was filled with puddles from the winter rains.

Of course we invited them in and were soon deep in discussion about the "new revelation of Jesus given in the Americas."

My interest in and study of the subject was a big help, yet I felt apprehensive as to whether they really had some secret weapon of doctrine or reasoning to support their claims.

Soon it became apparent that they were but boys, ill prepared for the job they were given to do. They had only had a couple of weeks of training and had been taught a canned presentation that had emphasized what to say and how to give "their" testimony.

Here in Douglas County began a trend that has manifested itself repeatedly over the years of my ministry. It was that Mrs. Crane felt sorry for these young boys who had no real clue about what they were trying to do. They were subjected to someone who had already spent several years studying their teachings. Usually they left befuddled and wondering if anything they had believed was true.

She once said after they had left, "I just felt so sorry for them, I wanted to bake them some cookies." The truth was they had no evidence to support their outlandish claims. She felt sorry for them to be sent out to be so embarrassed. Christians should be more open in talking with the LDS neighbors and friends, they can often be led to know the real Jesus.

In the years since, not one time have I met anyone, including those high up in the LDS church that could defend their claims. It is a system without foundation in fact.

A Mission President and University President

Mormon strategy has been to place their members in key positions in education, city, county, state and national government. This has proven very effective in giving this cultist church credibility and social acceptance.

Such was the case with Frank Jensen, professor in the university in a neighboring county to Douglas County. His name has been changed and the school not named because this bright man later left the LDS church and has since died.

I was asked to debate him at the University. The whole university was invited. The subject matter of the debate was finally agreed upon and our comments had to be limited to The Book of Mormon. The Bible could not be used. Frank said he was an expert in The Book of Mormon. With some feelings of uneasiness I agreed.

Each of us were to have two twenty-minute times for presentation with a ten minute time for refutation of what the other speaker said. Then at the conclusion each would have a fifteen-minute time to wrap up what was said.

Frank's first presentation was a typical Mormon recitation of unfounded claims and spurious affirmations. When I responded to him it was relatively easy to show the error of the Mormon claims.

During my initial presentation I discussed the problem the church had with the Book of Mormon having been translated by "the gift and power of God" and yet was filled with errors, an average of seven on each side of each page.

I continued by showing the absurdities of the narrative, such things as Nephi, one other man, two women and three boys building a sword factory, working in all manner of stone, wood, gold, sliver, bronze, steel, and precious stones, and building a temple like Solomon's. All of these tasks while establishing homes in the wilderness.

I pointed out the story of the cowboy snakes and boat with holes in the top and bottom, the matter of the brother of Jared and many other absurdities in the book. When these things were described, the audience frequently laughed at the foolishness of the Book.

Frank finally took his stand with the Book of Mormon because he had prayed and had a burning in his bosom. He agreed that much of it didn't make sense to him, but he accepted it by faith and a burning in the bosom.

I asked if he were sure the burning in his bosom had not been a case of indigestion. I stated that I had read the book, prayed and my mind had been enlightened to the many errors and fairy tales found in it.

Years passed, Frank began to study because questions had been raised in his mind. I lost track of him, but learned later that he had left the LDS church, even though he had been in charge of all mission work in the state, he left the church to accept Christ as Lord of his life. He later died of cancer in his mid fifties.

The ministry lends itself to many opportunities of teaching and influence that can change the lives of even those in superstition and cultist false teaching. Events like these make the life of ministers worthwhile and satisfying.

A Young Couple Seeks the Truth

After teaching a young couple for several weeks they asked, "Would you be willing to face anyone from the Mormon church to discuss these matters?"

I replied, "Certainly, bring anyone you want with you."

On the next Tuesday evening, low and behold if they didn't bring one of the very top apologists from the Utah headquarters. His job was to "defend the faith against Protestant ministers." As in earlier days, my feeling was, this time I have really gotten myself into it.

His initial statement was, "I have faced some of the best ministers across America and have confounded them all and have baptized several."

He bore all the marks of success and intelligence. We met at our home with the young couple. We sat around the kitchen table. He at one end, me at the other, the young couple one on each side. I had my stack of books and was as ready as time, information and prayer could make a person.

He was a skillful debater, the most knowledgeable Mormon I have ever met, and I had enough information to blow the doors off of the temple in Salt Lake City.

I took the offensive and began to discuss the vast changes in supposed revelations, changes in the Book of Mormon, Doctrine and Covenants, Pearl of Great Price and Joseph Smith's personal history. In each case I showed how the works claimed to be revelations that had been changed.

His look of calm assurance soon turned to one of concern. His voice turned from one filled with a sound of authority to uncertainty. He began to sweat, although it was cool in the house and no one else showed any signs of being too warm.

When he finally said he had just remembered that he had other things that he needed to be doing that evening, he had sweated so much that his light-colored dress shirt's collar was totally soaked, under his arms he had sweat till his shirt was wet clear down to his pants and he looked haggard and worn.

His parting comment to me before we got up from the table was, "If I knew as much about your church as you do about ours, I'm sure I could find just as many things wrong with it as you have with mine."

I assured him that my allegiance was only to the truth. If he or anyone else could show something false that I believed I was able to change my mind and adhere to the truth.

Because of encounters like these and hundreds of other similar to them, it appears the LDS people have been forbidden to talk with me. From this point on whenever I came to personally teach an LDS person no one was sent out from the church. It has been as if there was a rule that said, do not talk with Charles Crane.

An Old Seventh-Day Adventist

An old Seventh Day Adventist man, Hubert Jackman, often dropped into my office to give me some of their church writings. I found him a charming man and one who genuinely loved the Lord, though mistaught in several important doctrinal areas. We became good friends.

The phone rang one morning in my office and Hubert was on the line. He said, "Charles, I have an appointment with the Mormon missionaries this evening, would you come to help me?"

I replied, "Of course I would, but please don't tell them who I am. I will come in a pair of Levis and sport shirt and want you to introduce me as 'Chuck'."

That evening the missionaries showed a short movie. We both watched and after it was concluded Hubert asked several questions which they tried to answer.

I then asked if I could ask some questions. They readily agreed. After I asked them two or three questions the older missionary asked, "Are you Dr. Crane?"

I replied, "Yes."

They grabbed up their film, projector and left the house so fast that the cord from the projector was dragging behind them on the ground. Their parting words were, "We are not even supposed to talk with you."

Because of a life-long interest in the Mormon religion and the willingness to talk with them both publicly or privately, hundreds have become Christians.

Capstone Conference

Ed Decker, director of Ex-Mormons for Jesus, had been a friend for several years. He had left the LDS religion several years before and was seeking to win them to Christ.

Ed said, "Charles, could you give one of our keynote addresses at Capstone Conference this year?" I asked the date and what he expected. I agreed to come. The conference was to be held in the heart of Mormon country.

I flew in from Oregon and was picked up at the airport by taxi to be taken to where I was to catch a ride to the resort area. The taxi driver lost no time "bearing his testimony to me." He asked me why I was not a Mormon.

At the time Salt Lake City was having terrible flooding. Some of the streets were sand bagged and required detouring around them.

I asked him if it were true that when the Mormons came to the valley that Rocky Mountain, crickets almost wiped out their crops until the seagulls came and ate the crickets, saving the Mormons.

He assured me it was a true story.

I asked him, "Do you suppose God could get the seagulls to drink water?"

At Capstone, when it was time to speak there was such a huge crowd that it was necessary to video the speaker and show it in another large room where the overflow crowd was seated.

Right on the very front row was a very beautiful lady, seated with several other attractive people. I had no sooner gotten well into the material I was presenting on "A Text-Critical View of the Book of Mormon, when this lady got up hurriedly and rushed out.

My immediate thought was, that is the first Mormon I have offended. I was trying to be kind, but it did unsettle me some. But in about two minutes she came back in with a very handsome man with her and room was made for him on the very front row, almost in front of the podium.

At the conclusion of this over one-hour lecture he was the first to greet me. He introduced himself to me, "I'm Pat Matricianna and I am from Jeremiah Productions, a subsidiary of Burbank Film Studios of Hollywood, California. I am making a movie and you are exactly what is needed in it. Will you be a part?"

The next day filming took place most of the day and finally at about 10 p.m. I was called to talk about the Book of Mormon and archaeology. Really this isn't much to say, since this is no archaeological evidence for the Book of Mormon.

The film was made and titled *The God Makers*. It became one of the most often viewed religious movies of the year with millions of viewers. It resulted in such an exodus from the LDS church that it forced them to revise the excommunication process. Their Bishops were spending too much time in Bishop's courts to get their other work done.

Proverbs says, The person who becomes expert at their craft will stand before kings. When one chooses the ministry as a profession and gives diligence to that profession they will stand in positions of influence and honor. Certainly the ministry is one of life's highest callings.

The foundation continues to erode from under this monolithic cult. When will they give up the farce and return to mainstream Christianity? There are so many fine people, so many resources and now is the time to turn from what is false to the real Jesus and the true and living God. I pray this will happen soon.

Judge for Yourself

Each person will have to make their own judgment, but certainly the ministry, as a profession, could not be judged boring. People, variety, intellectual challenge, travel, thousands of friends, the chance for continual educational development, working with the finest people in a community, are but a few of the things that make me feel that the preaching ministry is the finest job in the whole world.

The medical doctor cares for the body, the teacher trains the mind, but the preacher deals with the soul of people, the only eternal part. God had only one Son and made Him a preacher of righteousness.

Yes, I suppose some preachers do look and act like they wear starched underwear, or sleep in a straight jacket. Yet, after over thirty years in the ministry I believe it is the finest job in the world.

Preachers, even though some do fail miserably, are the most moral, honest, trustworthy, people in any community. Blind studies find preachers the single most moral professional group in America and by a large margin. Still when someone has a serious problem their first reaction is to talk with their preacher.

In addition to this, the ministry is a profession that is never boring. There are those in season and out of season times that make every day different and interesting. If a person has the gifts, some do some do not, they should be preachers of Christ our Lord. Amen.

www.ingramcontent.com/pod-product-compliance
Lightning Source LLC
LaVergne TN
LVHW041617070426
835507LV00008B/305